Richard Skinner

Writing a Novel

**Bring your ideas to life
the Faber Academy way**

FABER & FABER

First published in 2018
by Faber & Faber Limited
Bloomsbury House
74–77 Great Russell Street
London WC1B 3DA

Typeset by Faber & Faber Limited
Printed and bound by CPI Group (UK) Ltd, Croydon, CRO 4YY

A CIP record for this book
is available from the British Library

ISBN 978-0-571-34046-0

MIX
Paper from
responsible sources
FSC® C020471
FSC
www.fsc.org

2 4 6 8 10 9 7 5 3 1

For my students

Contents

Preface

'There are three rules for writing the novel.
Unfortunately, no one knows what they are.'

W. SOMERSET MAUGHAM

The six-month Writing a Novel course at Faber Academy has successfully established itself since 2009 as one of the best writing courses in the world. The students range widely in age, nationality (Icelandic, Puerto Rican, Macedonian!) and background, but all who come to Faber Academy share the single recognition that writing, for them, is not simply an indulgence or hobby but a serious and profound force in their lives. The course does not aim to be a prescriptive approach to writing a novel, nor do we make any false promises of success. Instead, we aim to offer structure, guidance and support for each student to realise their potential as a writer and bring their work into being as fully as possible.

Soon after the start of the course, there is always a moment when the group bonds and 'takes off'. This is the happy point of no return; from then on, they start to work well as a group, learning to think and talk critically, learning to identify and articulate dilemmas and resolve them, for themselves and others, learning that every other writer's issue is also their own. For the duration of the course, they are equipping themselves as best they can for the rest of their lives as writers. In this way, the course places great emphasis on giving the students permission to write and to take themselves seriously as writers, and the confidence they gain as a result of this ethos is, perhaps, the best that we tutors can give to students. As a tutor, it is a pleasure and a privilege to be a part of that process and, without doubt, I learn just as much from the experience.

This book is the result of nearly twenty years' experience as a writer and creative writing tutor. I believe strongly in the ideas contained in it because they have helped me find my own way as a novelist. I have tried to share the knowledge and experience I have gained along the way, but I also want to encourage new writers to think about issues as they arise by means of lateral thinking, oblique strategies, aphorisms and quotations. I want to offer new writers a range of ideas about the art and craft of writing that stretches beyond the bounds of fiction. In this book, I cite many film references as well as using examples from fiction because, for me, film and fiction bear many similarities and share similar concerns. In the end, I do not believe that anyone can 'teach' another person how to write something as mysterious and magical as a novel. I believe the most a tutor can do is hold up a mirror to the students, make suggestions and point out the pitfalls along the way. Writing – and finishing – a novel is a difficult task, and you will encounter many dilemmas as you go, but I hope this book will help you to find the right solutions for yourself.

What is writing really about?

'What's writing really about? It's about trying to take fuller possession of the reality of your life.'

TED HUGHES

Students often ask me why I place so much emphasis on 'story' and not on the way a writer writes. The answer is a difficult one to articulate in a short time because to answer truthfully means that we have to grapple with the very notions of why we write. I believe the beginning of a writer's 'style' lies somewhere very deep inside oneself. Seamus Heaney described it thus: 'You are miming the real thing until one day the chain draws unexpectedly tight and you have dipped into the waters that will continue to entice you back. You have broken the skin on the pool of yourself.'

> I believe the beginning of a writer's 'style' lies somewhere very deep inside oneself

A writer's style is not just to do with the basic practical choices a writer makes about how to write; it is also to do with something more intimate, or even philosophical, than that. It is closely wed to notions of perception, personality, morality and possibility; it is tied to the choices we make in life. In your writing, readers should be able to hear the contents of your heart, your mind and your soul.

So, if a writer's 'style' is the sum and signature of their personality, then a writer's true biography amounts to no more than the story of their style. And when we talk about a writer's style, what we are actually talking about is their 'voice', which is something that a writer can only discover for themselves in, and over, time. A writer's voice is the deepest reflection of who they are and this is absolutely not something anyone can, or should, 'teach'.

As a tutor, I can do nothing about the tone of your voice as you speak, but what I *can* engage with is what you say, i.e. your 'story'. The elements of good storytelling *are* something that can be discussed, examined, tested, moulded, learned. Underneath any amount of layering of tone and texture there should be a rock solid story. A writer's first business is to decide: what's going to happen? To whom? When? Where? Once you have your story, you need to decide in what order you are going to place those events. Putting them in different orders will create different effects.

Plotting is finding the desire lines in your story, the path of least resistance

Plotting is finding the desire lines in your story, the path of least resistance. By thinking through your story again and again, you become more and more familiar with it, knowing better and better for yourself how it should be told. Discuss, examine, test, mould, learn and ask again and again: 'Where's the story? Where's the story?'

Ask yourself this question and it is like standing in a stream – although you can't see it, you can feel its current on your ankles, can't you? You can see ahead of you how the stream runs. To get to know the structure of your story is to feel the direction of the current and to go with the flow. To dip into the waters of yourselves.

Creating ideas
Where do ideas come from?

'We do not choose our subjects. They choose us.'

GUSTAVE FLAUBERT

Stories are not written from the head or the heart, they are written from the stomach. This is one of the strongest beliefs I have about writing. An idea comes to mind, one which you love and think would be a great idea for a novel and you plan to start writing straightaway. But a good idea needs much more time than that to develop and grow. It needs time to sink further into your body, until it assimilates itself into your very being. So, when you think you have a good idea for a novel – *wait*. You do not write a good novel by over-thinking it or falling in love with it too much – you should start writing only when you have a good gut feeling about it. The longer you wait, the quicker and more fully formed your story will come out.

Stories are not written from the head or the heart, they are written from the stomach

Novels come together in this way, rather like planets – ideas slowly amass and gradually coalesce to form something that has weight. It is hard to know when a novel 'starts' and your self ends. In his essay 'Tradition and the Individual

Talent', T. S. Eliot described this process as: 'When a filament of platinum is introduced into a chamber containing oxygen and sulphur dioxide . . . they form sulphurous acid. This combination takes place only if the platinum is present; nevertheless the newly formed acid contains no trace of platinum, and the platinum itself is apparently unaffected; has remained inert, neutral, and unchanged. The mind of the poet is the shred of platinum.'

For writers, unlike chemists, it is impossible to know with certainty if or when this sort of reaction will happen. There is no DIY manual that guarantees success, and if any 'how to write a novel' book makes such a promise, it is not to be trusted. A novel is not a machine that you put together according to a set of instructions, as you would build a Range Rover, or solve a Rubik's cube – it is a mystical, magical object whose creation is the result of processes that remain largely unknowable and unpredictable to its author. We are all just the platinum.

So, if we cannot initiate this process ourselves, what else can we do? Well, I believe there is a fundamental question writers can ask themselves before ever putting pen to paper – just what is it that you want to write about, what is it you want to *say*? Despite not being able to control fully how ideas are created, you can help coax them into being by asking yourself what it is you care most passionately and deeply about. All books begin with an idea, a spark, a seed – what Henry James called a *donnée*.

'You know that phrase "What is the elephant in the room?" What is the elephant in your novel?'

DEBORAH LEVY

A good place to start to think about what it is you want to say in your own writing is to look at the kinds of stories you like. Off the top of your head, make a list of ten books that have moved you the most profoundly. Are there any common themes? Almost certainly there will be. Why do you think that is? Any themes you do find are clearly those that touch your heart the deepest and so are probably what you should be exploring in your own writing. Andrew Motion, my MA Creative Writing tutor at UEA, once commented that a short story of mine was about 'invisible others', a comment that hit me right between the eyes. In light of this comment, I thought a great deal about my reasons for wanting to write and why I was drawn to certain books. He was right, of course, and I have never forgotten this insight into my work.

Another way of posing the same question is to ask yourself what kind of book you would write if you knew for sure that it would *not* be published. If there were no pressure or expectation on you, what would you produce? This is a good approach to take because it emphasises the point that if the central idea in a novel is one you care passionately and deeply about, one that is very close to your heart, you stand a much better chance of actually getting a whole first draft out. The first person you should be writing for is yourself.

> 'A work of art is good if it has sprung from necessity.'
> RAINER MARIA RILKE

A novel worth writing should hold you to ransom. Paul Auster, perhaps still best known for his debut novel *The New York Trilogy*, is a good case in point. Most people think of it as his first book, but there is a book he wrote beforehand, entitled *The Invention of Solitude*, which is an intensely personal piece of life writing. The first half is subtitled 'Portrait of an Invisible Man' and is a study of his father, who almost certainly had Asperger's syndrome. The second half, subtitled 'The Book of Memory', is to do with Auster's feelings about becoming a father himself. Auster wrote the first half as a response to the death of his father, so the two halves – death and birth – are mirror images, with Auster himself in the middle. The second half was, Auster says, particularly difficult to write: 'the more deeply I descended into the material, the more distanced I became from it'. He solved the problem, he says, by treating himself as though he were someone else and re-writing the piece in the third person. The book was a way of 'clearing his throat'; the piece he felt compelled to write before he could go on to write anything else.

A novel worth writing should hold you to ransom

Extensive vs intensive reading

Reading and writing are two sides of the same coin, but it is not only what you read that is important, it is *how* you read, too. When starting to read a novel for the first time, or re-reading an old favourite, try to view it as an editor would, looking 'through' the text in X-ray fashion, as it were. Reading books in this way allows you to examine a narrative closely, locating and identifying deep structure and embedded themes. How does the writer bring their themes to life? What most appealed to you about the story? How was that dramatised in the narrative? Try to begin reading not just for pleasure, but also for ideas. Reading in this way can be a great source of inspiration and you should not hesitate to use all this stimulation and motivation to kick-start your own work.

> '*A work is eternal not because it imposes a single meaning on different men, but because it suggests different meanings to a single man.*'
>
> ROLAND BARTHES

Of course, it is good to read as widely as possible – especially outside your race, class and gender – but, as a writer, I have found that returning to the same book many times over can be just as, if not more, instructive. When you finish reading a novel for the first time, your memory of it does not stay fixed forever; it shifts and evolves. Years later, you might find yourself talking about it, only to discover that your memory has retained just a few scraps – mythic representations – of the text. You realise that, in the intervening years, you have reconstructed in your mind an entirely different book – an inner book of 'received beliefs' – from the actual one. This is when the value of re-reading becomes obvious. A book comes alive with each new reading. A book is born again every time you pick it up. When you re-read a book, it will appear to be different on a second or third reading, but of course the book has not changed, you have. Any text has the potential for several different interpretations, and no one reading can ever exhaust a text's full potential because, on re-reading, each reader will search for connections in their own way, excluding other possibilities and thus making them aware of their own role in the play of meaning. It is not the case that subsequent readings are any 'truer' than the first – they are just different. The fact that readers can be differently affected by the same text shows the degree to which reading is a creative process. If you read a single book many times over, it marks the changes in your life and, whatever happens, you continue to have a conversation with it.

Reading is a creative process

Paul Bowles' *The Sheltering Sky* is a novel that I happen to have read a number of times and, each time I re-read it, it offers fresh insights into how and why I think it is such a great piece of work. Set in North Africa just after the Second World War, the novel is about husband and wife Port and

Kit, and their travels after they arrive in Tangier. When I first read the novel, I thought it was Port's story, but after a few more reads I realised it was, in fact, Kit's. She is the character who undergoes the most change and the person in whose company we end the story. Also, I had not noticed at first how Port and Kit's journey starts at the coast, in a well-populated city, and goes directly inland, stopping at places that become fewer and further between and less and less well populated until, ultimately, they arrive in the middle of nowhere. This doomed journey into the desert is a subtle, sophisticated metaphor for their relationship. I also had not noticed that, although Port and Kit both have sexual encounters with native Arabs, it is how they respond to those encounters that matters, that defines the difference between their personalities. Port's is a one-night stand and the experience 'poisons' him and is his ultimate undoing. Kit, on the other hand, enters into a desperate, very physical affair with a Bedouin that rejuvenates her body entirely and sets her off on another journey altogether.

Imitation

> *'Talent borrows but genius steals.'*
>
> T. S. ELIOT

Take a favourite novel (perhaps from your list of ten), open it at random and copy out a page from it. Do this by hand: that way you claim ownership of it and so it will feel a little bit like your own writing. Have a look at the flow of sentences. What struck you as you were copying out the passage? Write down any devices, effects or tricks the author uses. The point of this exercise is to show you that imitating good writing like this can be a good way into your own work, since counterfeiting is very close to invention.

Imagine listening to a Chopin nocturne – fifteen minutes of sheer beauty. But then imagine if I asked you to play it yourself; you would have to approach it in a completely different way. Now, you are not so concerned about its beauty, you are thinking more about where you have to place your fingers in order to play it. This teaches you that the 'necessity' of writing comes way before its beauty. When you start writing your novel, do not tell yourself you are going to write a beautiful novel – just concentrate on the simple ABCs of storytelling. Leave its beauty to others.

> **The 'necessity' of writing comes way before its beauty**

Improvisation

Another option is, of course, just to write, to start writing without giving any thought to it at all. For some writers, it is only in the act of writing that ideas are generated. Try this: write for ten minutes about an old friend. Just write what immediately comes to mind; do not think about it too much. Then write for another ten minutes about what you did yesterday. Finally, write for another ten minutes making a link between the two. Did you find a link? If you did, the third paragraph will almost certainly contain a very good idea. If you do not think you did, look again. There is always a link because you are the link. Writing automatically like this bypasses the conscious mind and gives us direct access to the subconscious, where many good ideas can lurk but where we do not usually look. Good writing is about 'mess', so don't censor yourself. The best novels are about the mess human beings make. An overly polite, neat and tidy book will almost certainly be dull.

I have used this exercise many times in classes with great success. The ideas that the exercise drags up never fail to surprise students. It is useful because it is rather like the whole writing process in miniature – in those first two parts, you are using raw, seemingly banal material and then using cross-fertilisation to create something new. You are rubbing things together to create a spark, the *donnée*. Good writing is not about copying the world around you, it's about creating something out of nothing. It's that *something* we're all after; it's the juice.

> *Good writing is not about copying the world around you, it's about creating something out of nothing*

Good practice

So far, we have talked about favourite novels and common themes, about reading widely and deeply, about imitating and improvising as a way of generating ideas – these are all things you can do on your own at your desk, but can you generate ideas when you are 'on the go'?

Yes, of course you can.

The first, and most obvious, thing is to keep a notebook on you at all times and to use it often. Write down anything that pops into your mind. If you treat this notebook as an extension of your thought processes, you will find yourself returning to it repeatedly. I have been keeping notebooks ever since I can remember, using them to store ideas that come to mind at the most unexpected moments, and that would evaporate into the ether just as quickly if they were not written down: snippets of conversation, quotations, words whose meaning I do not know, diagrams, postcards, leaflets, lists, reviews, aphorisms. During the early stages of thinking through and planning a novel, I find myself consulting these notebooks endlessly, picking out ideas and checking that I am on the right track. They are among my most treasured, irreplaceable possessions.

I also trawl through newspapers and magazines, tearing out and keeping anything of interest. After many years of storing such articles, I decided to impose some kind of order on my huge cache. I soon found that many of them were about related subjects and I started to file them according to subject matter, compiling a dozen or so folders: one was labelled 'Consciousness, Einstein, Bergson, Maths, Morality, Desire'; another was labelled 'Amnesia, Dementia, Depression, Bereavement, Memory, Mapping, Types of Love, Living Alone'; and a third was labelled 'Missing People,

Recluses, Murder, Suicide, Zombies, Adversaries, Rose West, Myra Hindley'. I realised that each of these folders potentially had enough material in it for a novel.

Other people's life stories are a fabulous resource for you. George Bernard Shaw defined a writer as someone who is 'half vivisector, half vampire'. Good writers have a sixth sense about people, an interest in human nature that borders on the morbid, so always have your antennae up. Some of the most interesting stories I have heard have been told to me in passing. The origins of my novel *The Darks* lay in two stories I heard, one from a TV documentary and the other told at a dinner party by a stranger. These two stories – about a woman who has visions and a man who has blackouts – were both remarkable in themselves, but when put together, they were irresistible.

'Tentative d'épuisement d'un lieu parisien'

One of my greatest pleasures, and sources of ideas, is going to a crowded place – a railway station or a café – and just taking in what is happening around me. People-watching is fascinating because it gives you huge numbers of visual stimuli to help you invent and build stories about the strangers around you. You could take this process a step further and write these sketches and short stories there and then, a process that will improve your powers of observation and description enormously.

One overcast weekend in October 1974, the French

writer Georges Perec spent three days at a café in Place Saint-Sulpice, Paris, recording everything that passed through his field of vision: the people walking by; the buses and school cars caught up in their routes; the pigeons moving en masse; a wedding (and then a funeral) at the church in the centre of the square; the signs, symbols and slogans littering everything; and the darkness that eventually absorbs it all. He called this exercise *'Tentative d'épuisement d'un lieu parisien'*, which translates as 'An attempt at exhausting a Parisian location'. His book is an eerie, oddly touching document, and is a wonderful exercise in such observation and description.

While I was in Malaga in the winter of 2012, I spent a couple of hours one morning on the Calle Marqués de Larios observing an elderly man sitting at a café. He was about seventy years old, very smartly turned out in an olive green check jacket, green slacks, brown brogues, a white shirt and cerise tie. He had little hair, but it was neatly cut and combed. He wore metal-framed glasses and had a hangdog expression and hunched shoulders. He was obviously retired and I decided that he must have been an accountant, or an insurance man – something to do with finance. He was sitting at a well-known café called Lepanto, watching the world go by, but studiously ignoring the jazz band that was playing for money on the street nearby. He was a man who enjoyed peace and quiet. He was joined by a lady of a similar age whom, I quickly realised, he had been expecting. She wore a grey ruffled cotton jacket and smart blue jeans. Her hair was auburn (dyed?) and her glasses were tinted orange. They immediately launched into debate, though I was too far away to hear, and I understood that he enjoyed other people's company more than I thought he would. They seemed familiar, intimate with each other, and I thought that maybe they had once been lovers. I imagined them as characters in a Gabriel García Márquez short story. Perhaps they were childhood friends who had been lovers and now were only friends again. Once passionate with each other, they were now too old to be bothered with the trials and tribulations of love.

After some time, she kissed him goodbye and left. He paid the bill and walked in the other direction. I followed him. He was carrying a shopping bag that I had not noticed before. He had been shopping for clothes. He walked slowly and had a habit of pulling on his lapels. Out of his right-hand pocket, he pulled a handkerchief, which he carried in his left hand. He stopped to talk to a man selling lottery tickets in the street, then went into a tobacconist's and bought several tickets. He then went into a shop further up the street that sold huge rolls of fabric, all different colours and patterns, and it struck me that maybe he had worked in the fashion business, perhaps as a dressmaker. This would account for his smartly dressed appearance and the shopping bag. At this point I stopped following him and watched as he left the fabric shop, crossed a square and disappeared down an alleyway. He was a fabulous character and I have never forgotten him.

'Qualia'

When in public spaces, listening is also key. What do you hear? How could you combine the sounds to make a story? What can you smell? In fiction, smell is by far the most overlooked of the senses. The visual aspect tends to dominate, but you should employ as many of the senses as possible in your writing. What can you taste? Or touch? What can you smell?

'Qualia' is the scientific term for specific instances of our subjective experience of the world – the smell of coffee, for instance, or the sound of a waterfall. Think back to a good holiday you have had: what are the strongest sensory impressions you remember? The burning sand on a beach? The heat of the sun? The colour of a material? The taste of a local dish? Looking at the scene in front of you via sensory impressions like these will help you to see it more directly, as if for the first time. Familiarity is a great deadener, so take yourself to an unfamiliar place and ask yourself what it is about a tree that makes it a tree, or, to quote Viktor Shklovsky, what makes 'the stone *stony*'. These 'qualia' are among the essential ingredients of fiction; they can bring a character, a scene or a setting to life, so learn to look for them, especially where there seem to be none.

Process vs product

'Storytelling began as ceremony and evolved into ritual.'
PAUL SCHRADER

Spinning yarns is as much about the spinning as it is about the yarn – about process as much as product – and good writing is the result of endless practice. No one is going to write your novel for you, so you have to develop the discipline to get the writing done. When you are not in the mood, when you are feeling low or when the weather's gorgeous, slaving away at a desk is not always an inviting prospect. Describing how she felt most mornings when faced with the task of writing, Susan Sontag said it was much like jumping into an icy lake – horrible at first, but fine once you got moving. This process can seem interminably slow at times. A sentence here, a section there – it hardly seems worth it – but bear in mind that what actually appears on the page is just the tip of the iceberg. Those hours of thinking, doubting, clarifying, rejecting, rethinking are all part of the process.

Your task as a writer is not to learn lots of techniques, but to learn some simple ones – and to learn them as perfectly as you can. With practice, the process of writing becomes more familiar. The writing itself always remains difficult, no matter how experienced you are, but familiarity with the process means that you become better at knowing instinctively when things are going right or wrong. Gradually, the difficult becomes easier, the easy becomes more habitual, and the habitual becomes beautiful.

Walter Benjamin said that writing had three phases: the musical when it is composed; the architectural when it is built; and the textile when it is woven. You are at this compositional phase now. The main point at this stage is to try to let any ideas come naturally – if you force them, they will elude you. The best ideas are those that are received rather than sought.

The best ideas are those that are received rather than sought

Be patient, remain empty. Read as much as you can, letting it feed into your work. Exercise your writing as much as possible in order to write well when the time comes, just as a musician practises scales or an artist sketches in order to be ready to do the work. Stay focused – discipline is what will translate your talent into ability. Keep your nerve, keep the courage of your convictions. And when you have a hunch? Go for it.

'Act boldly and unseen forces will come to your aid.'
DOROTHEA BRANDE

Planning
How do you set about starting to write?

When an idea for a novel has presented itself, your next task is to find a way of formulating it. Not only do you have to get the size of a story right, but the measure of it, too. This is often the most daunting part of writing, and it is at this point when many give up. Planning helps you to disclose the vision you have in mind via a text that is yet to come. If you do not plan, your first attempts at writing a novel will feel 'provisional'; with a plan, on the other hand, you have a safety net as you embark on the risky act of writing a first draft. You are at Benjamin's 'architectural' phase now; you have let the imaginative, creative part of your mind do its work – now you have to build your novel, bit by bit, step by step.

Sustainment and development

One of the most challenging issues for new writers is the formidable task of writing something as long as a novel. And one of the things I see happen very often with new writers is that, when they have a good idea for a novel, they start writing far too early. The result of this is what I call 'front ending'. The temptation for new writers is to pile all the 'story' into the first few chapters so that there is a car crash of events in the first fifty or so pages and then the novel runs out of steam. Eager and impatient to start, many new writers fail to see that these events have to be

Twist your plot like a screw, don't hammer it like a nail

spread out evenly along the narrative, like pearls on a necklace, so that the story is sustained, and they fail to see that a novel has to change and grow and develop. These are two key issues for new writers: sustainment and development of theme. Sustainment ensures that the story does not sag; development makes certain that the story changes. You have to keep the story up in the air and yet, at the same time, you have to constantly move it forward. This balancing act feels counterintuitive – it feels more like a juggling act – and is one of the most difficult things to pull off as a writer. If you want to build a story that will last, twist your plot like a screw, don't hammer it like a nail. In a narrative, time exists in order that everything does not happen at once and space exists so that it does not only happen in one place. Make full use of both to sustain and develop your novel.

> _'Plot might seem to be a matter of choice. It is not. It is what is left after the whittling away of alternatives.'_
> ELIZABETH BOWEN

If you are the kind of planner who benefits from preparing for a project before embarking on it, you might find it useful to go through your story visually. A simple way to start planning is to list the numbers 1 to 30 on a piece of paper. On average, a novel will have thirty chapters, so each number will correspond to a chapter of your book. Adjacent to number 1, note down your opening scene, and your closing scene next to number 30.

When you are going over what will take place in the middle of your story, keep in mind the overarching structure of the classic three-act drama: the first act is the 'situation'; the second act is the 'complication'; and the third act is the 'resolution'. In Hollywood terminology, Act I is the 'set-up', Act II is the 'conflict' and Act III is the 'pay-off'. Numbers 1 to 5 or 6 should set up the story, and the denouement should correspondingly happen across scenes 24 or 25 to 30. Write down the key events in your story next to the middle numbers. Move them around until you find an order that brings out the best in your story. Playing with form in this way can help to shape thoughts and clarify feelings and, with practice, this play can turn into a pursuit of excellence through a fulfilment of targets.

You keep the reader's attention not by giving them information, but by withholding it from them

In terms of providing answers at the end of your story to the questions posed at its beginning, this structure should read as a continual process of elimination. The first act should show that the story could move in any number of directions, the second act should narrow these possibilities down and show that only some directions are probable, while the final act should move towards one outcome being inevitable. Doing this is like playing a game of hide and seek with the reader – you need to give the reader enough to keep their attention but not so much that you give the game away. Remember, you keep the reader's attention not by giving them information, but by withholding it from them. The desire to find out what happens next is what keeps the reader glued to the page.

> 'It is easy to plant clues and make a reasonable story out of three seemingly unconnected facts because the author is working backwards.'
>
> JOHN BUCHAN

With genre fiction, particularly when the storyline ends definitely and unambiguously (crime novels, for instance), ordering scenes in this way will help enormously. If you are still having problems working out the chronology, however, take Buchan's advice literally – start at the end and plot your story backwards. Breaking down your novel into bits of time like this will help you to overcome the magnitude of the task ahead.

When American writer Chester Himes arrived in Paris in the 1950s, he was hired by the founder of the Série Noire crime imprint, Marcel Duhamel, to write a crime novel. Himes complained that he had no idea how to write a crime novel, so Duhamel gave him some advice, which, although seemingly offhand, is actually great:

Get an idea. Start with action, somebody does something – a man reaches out a hand and opens a door, light shines in his eyes, a body lies on the floor, he turns, looks up and down the hall. Action always in detail. Make pictures. Like motion pictures. Always the scenes are visible. No stream of consciousness at all. We don't give a damn who's thinking what – only what they're doing. Always doing something. From one scene to another. Don't worry about it making sense . . . That's for the end . . . Keep the suspense going. Don't let your people talk too much. Use the dialogue for narration, like Hammett. Have your people see the description. You stay out of it.

Himes followed Duhamel's advice and produced countless crime novels for the imprint, eventually winning France's Grand Prix de Littérature Policière in 1958.

'I start with a tingle, a kind of feeling of the story I will write. Then come the characters, and they take over, they make the story. All this ends by being a plot.'

KAREN BLIXEN

Although some planning undoubtedly helps aspiring novelists, it is not the case that you must have your story planned and perfectly plotted before putting pen to paper. In fact, it is a good idea to leave room for manoeuvre since better ideas might come up along the way. Make allowances for that and do not be afraid to follow them wherever they may take you. Usually, a writer will use a bit of both. Here is Paul Bowles:

> Every work suggests its own method. Each novel's been done differently, under different circumstances and using different methods. I got the idea for *The Sheltering Sky* riding on a Fifth Avenue bus one day going uptown from Tenth Street. I decided just which point of view I would take. It would be a work in which the narrator was omniscient. I would write it consciously up to a certain point, and after that let it take its own course. You remember there's a little Kafka quote at the beginning of the third section: 'From a certain point onward there is no longer any turning back; that is the point that must be reached.' This seemed important to me, and when I got to that point, beyond which there was no turning back, I decided to use a surrealist technique – simply writing without any thought of what I had already written, or awareness of what I was writing, or intention as to what I was going to write next, or how it was going to finish. And I did that.

With fiction that is less generic, more 'literary', it is perfectly viable to start *in medias res* because you are never entirely sure how the story is going to unfold. In the planning of such fiction, you are confronted by a fair number of possibilities and, sometimes, the best thing to do is just to go for one with a quick decision and then make that particular choice work for you. It takes you to interesting places with surprising results.

The ending

Endings bring a resolution to an enigma, relief to suspense and clarity to confusion, before transporting the reader from the text back out into the real world. A lot of 'classic' books are conventionally moral, with their ends in their beginnings; they are 'classic' texts, referring back on themselves and offering us a closed-circuit view of the world. Typically, they display a strong linearity of cause and effect, and there is a high degree of narrative 'closure'. Alain Robbe-Grillet described the nineteenth-century novel as a 'system' of 'cumbersome machinery of continuity, linear chronology, causal sequences, non-contradiction'. These are books one can indeed judge by their covers.

The endings of some Modernist and Postmodern texts do not guarantee such a secure moral world quite so emphatically. For a start, the narration of events in the story might not be organised according to cause and effect, so that the narrative may be highly digressive or appear to take wrong turns. Also, narrative 'closure' may be problematic or ambiguous; questions set up early in the narrative might be left unanswered, for example, or matters left hanging. These kinds of texts can have meaning but no point. They simply do not add up. They prefer aperture to closure – the comma, minor key and the cliffhanger over perfect cadences, happy endings and full stops.

They prefer aperture to closure – the comma, minor key and the cliffhanger over perfect cadences, happy endings and full stops

'A work of art should also be "an object difficult to pick up". The less it's understood, the slower it opens its petals, the later it will fade.'

JEAN COCTEAU

What kind of writer are you?

'Writing a novel is like embarking on [a crossing of] the Atlantic in a canoe; after weeks of paddling you can't see the land that you left, but the other shore will not come into sight for months, or even years.'

ELIZABETH JANE HOWARD

Apparently, everyone has a novel inside them, but very few manage to arrange themselves and their lives well enough to get it out. You, however, have decided on a plan of action and are now ready to set out on this journey. To start a novel, you have to be ready, able and willing, but to finish a novel, you have to have staying power. John Gardner compared writing a novel to running a marathon rather than a sprint. A sprint is a concentrated burst of energy; but to run a marathon you need a strategy, cunning, flexibility, timing. But most of all, you need stamina.

As with any job, it is essential to find out the best working practices to smooth your progress as a writer. Are you a night owl or a morning lark, for instance? Virginia Woolf could only write in the mornings; Keats only with a clean shirt on; Ernest Hemingway only wrote standing up; Paul

Bowles could only write in bed. The point is that you should find your own *modus operandi* as a writer. Settling as quickly as possible into a routine that suits your temperament will allow you to produce the most work of the best possible quality.

'Eker' or 'gusher'?

All writers fall into two categories: either you are an 'eker' or a 'gusher'. I have also seen them called 'plotters' and 'pantsers', and George R. R. Martin refers to them as 'architects' and 'gardeners'. Do you like to 'binge write'? To sit down in one long session and allow your work to issue forth? To 'gush' without impediment? With this very organic approach, the quality of your work, for now, matters much less than the quantity. What is important is to get everything out, and to do so in any order – the task of editing and rewriting can come much later. The important thing here is to keep on going, not to stop until you have a first draft.

Alternatively, you may prefer to set aside a small amount of time every day and 'eke' out a set number of words. This is a much more methodical, mechanical approach. Some writers are even known to stop dead on their target, even though they might be midway through a scene and know exactly how to continue with it. When asked how much one should write every day, Hemingway replied, 'always stop when you are going good and when you know what will happen next. If you do that every day when you are writing a novel you will never be stuck.' The advantage is that this approach is not nearly so 'exhaustive'; each sitting takes much less out of you, so you have more energy for the following day.

Apropos this difference, Leonard Cohen tells a story about the time he found himself in Paris on the same evening as Bob Dylan was performing there. After the concert, he and Dylan met and had a conversation about the different ways they wrote songs. Cohen told Dylan that he had just finished writing a song called 'Hallelujah', and he sang the last verse to Dylan, saying that it was 'a rather joyous song' (it is not). Cohen went on to explain that writing it had been difficult and had taken him two years. This shocked Dylan, who pointed out that his average writing time for a song was no more than fifteen minutes. Cohen was speechless. Dylan must have liked 'Hallelujah', however, as it is one of the few songs written by someone else that he has performed live.

Montage vs mise-en-scène

In 1956, the French film theorist André Bazin set up a two-fold distinction in film style: *montage vs mise-en-scène*. *'Montage'* is the French word for the editing process in film, the cutting together of shots – literally the 'mounting' of the shots. *'Mise-en-scène'*, on the other hand, literally means 'arranging things in the shot', and is the French equivalent of 'direction'. Bazin believed passionately that films should not be made according to some *a priori* plan but that they should be made from bits of reality whose meaning could only be understood *a posteriori*.

In terms of fiction, this dichotomy can be summarised as the difference between keeping sentences short and crisp, preferring to generate meaning in the accumulation of sentences, and allowing a sentence to expand in order to accommodate a number of images and ideas chosen to generate meaning within a single sentence. In the former, meaning exists *between* sentences, not *in* them. It says that, although a single sentence is grammatically complete, it is narratively incomplete. It is the *combination* of sentences that is a narrative statement. In the latter, however, there is an 'objective reality' inherent *within* the single sentence that does not exist outside it. The link between sentences is weak here; it is the *selection* of images that is important, not the combination.

> '*Sentences are factual, but paragraphs are emotional.*'
>
> GERTRUDE STEIN

The metaphoric and metonymic poles

In the same year as Bazin created his distinction, the Russian formalist Roman Jakobson arrived at a similar dichotomy by looking at the concepts of metaphor and metonymy. He began by outlining the two basic principles and operations of language: selection and combination. In a sentence like 'Ships crossed the ocean', I select from a set of words and then combine them to produce a meaning. If I substitute 'ploughed' for 'crossed', I have created a metaphor based on a similarity between things that are otherwise different. If I substitute 'deep' for 'sea', I have used metonymy, which uses attributes or effects of a thing to signify that thing. Metaphor operates along an axis of language that Jakobson calls the 'selection', whereas metonymy operates along the 'combination' axis. Jakobson develops this idea by going on to propose that metonymy is the general overriding principle in Realism (citing the moment in Tolstoy's *Anna Karenina* when our attention is focused on Anna's handbag at the scene of her suicide), whereas Romanticism is 'closely linked to metaphor'.

Hemingway and Proust provide good illustrations of these differences. Hemingway's early writing consists of using short, crisp sentences that describe single, complete actions. In isolation, no one sentence carries much meaning other than the purely descriptive. With Proust, however, the sentences tend to be much longer, filled with clauses and sub-clauses marked off by semi-colons, whose significance grows so much that it almost tells a story within itself. We might say that Hemingway's style is founded on *montage*, while Proust's is rooted in *mise-en-scène*.

Hemingway's style is founded on montage, while Proust's is rooted in mise-en-scène

Hemingway himself once advised a writer to 'take out all the beautiful words and see if it still works'. The idea is that the less loaded the sentence, or 'shot', the more powerful the juxtaposition of two sentences, or 'cut'. A blue beside a green is not the same blue as when it is placed beside a yellow, or a red. Not surprisingly, Sergei Eisenstein – the high priest of *montage* – posited a similar idea, which he termed the '*montage* of attractions', by which he meant that what precedes the cut should attract what follows it, and *vice versa*. The energy of this attraction could derive from a contrast, a comparison or a repetition. In this way, the 'cut' acts like the hinge of a metaphor.

*'The fox knows many things, but the hedgehog knows
one big thing.'*

ARCHILOCHUS

When all is said and done, however, you can no more impose a style on yourself than you can force a story. Your writing style will emerge in, and over, time. If 'style' is the signature of a writer's will, then a writer's true biography should amount to no more than the story of their style. Some writers go to great lengths to suppress style by purposefully adopting wildly differing genres for each new book, preferring the genre, not the writer themselves, to express whatever it is the writer wants to say. Conversely, other writers use each new book as an opportunity to develop their own particular writing style, a worldview that is deeply personal and intimate, almost as if all their books were actually one huge book.

But, for now, do not even think about the marketplace. Instead, concentrate all your time and effort into planning well and getting your narrative off the ground. If you are keeping an eye on the market at this early stage, you will take one eye off the ball. Equally, try not to write *for* the marketplace. If you follow a plot blueprint that many others have used a thousand times before, not only will your story lack originality, but it will come across as too 'on the nose'. Write the kind of book you would like to read, but also try to make it your own.

A book is a maze and you might sometimes find that you have taken a wrong turn, or made a false start, or come to a dead end. All writers know where they have gone wrong, really. Deep down. Consult your plan, go back to the place you got lost and re-route yourself. Sometimes you may get so lost that you have to throw work away. This can, of course, be dispiriting, but you learn just as much from a novel that does not work as from one that does. The lesson is just as valuable. There is nothing to be done except to pick yourself up, dust yourself down, and move on.

All writers know where they have gone wrong, really. Deep down.

Print out and pin up a plan of how much writing to do every day/week/month and work to your deadlines. Focus on the day-to-day, and soon you will find weeks have slipped by and you are well into the first draft. At the same time, ensure your targets are realistic: if you aim too high, you will almost certainly fail and feel disheartened; on the other hand, if you aim too low, you will feel that you are not fulfilling your potential. There is nothing like the feel-

ing of a job well done, so work yourself hard but take care
not to make appointments your abilities cannot keep.

'Write a little every day, without hope or despair.'
ISAK DINESEN

Character
For many writers, character is the holy grail. But what is character?

What is character? A friend once said to me that idiosyncrasy is the mother of all character and description the father, which, while not strictly a definition, is as good an effort as I have ever heard. When it comes to writing fiction, this question is mind-boggling. Creating a character seems like such a difficult task, one that has no obvious starting or end point. It seems impossible to achieve without recourse to voodoo. So, just how does a character on paper become a living, breathing citizen, walking and talking and acting in the world?

> *Idiosyncrasy is the mother of all character and description the father*

'Outside in'

One ruse is to start from the 'outside in'. Start with a few basic biographical details, such as age, star sign, occupation, interests. Create and fill out questionnaires for your characters, listing these basic details but also going into much greater detail about their habits, peccadillos, distinguishing features, political views. Make a 'mood board' for them – a collection of images, texts and objects that you feel represent them or say something about their personality.

Another trick to get started is to make a list of the first ten objects that come to mind and create a character out of as many of them as possible. It might seem like a trivial exercise, but you can tell a lot about someone by what they have on their person or in their home. In his collection of stories about Vietnam, *The Things They Carried*, Tim O'Brien starts by listing the things he and his fellow soldiers carried through necessity, things that comment very eloquently on the dangers, reduced circumstances and boredom of life as a grunt, and that make immediately apparent the differences between the men:

> P-38 can openers, pocket knives, heat tabs, wristwatches, dog tags, mosquito repellent, chewing gum, candy, cigarettes, salt tablets, packets of Kool-Aid, lighters, matches, sewing kits, Military Payment Certificates, C rations, and two or three canteens of water. Together, these items weighed between 15 and 20 pounds, depending on a man's habits or rate of metabolism. Henry Dobbins, who was a big man, carried extra rations; he was especially fond of canned peaches in heavy syrup over pound cake. Dave Jensen, who practiced field hygiene, carried a toothbrush, dental floss, and several hotel-sized bars of soap he'd stolen on R&R in Sydney, Australia. Ted Lavender, who was scared, carried tranquilizers until he was shot in the head outside the village of Than Khe in mid-April.

Another way to approach a character is via their name. Consider 'Luke Skywalker'. The first thing you notice about the name is how regal it sounds – a man who walks in the sky – which is perfectly fitting as he discovers during the course of *Star Wars* that he is indeed a prince. But there are other qualities about the name that comment on his character. Luke was an apostle, for instance, and the biblical name conjures ideas of honesty, virtue and truth. Then there is the alliteration – those three plosive 'k' sounds are hard, strong, which implies that this man means business, that he is not to be messed with. The name 'Madame Bovary' summons up two key ideas: the book is called *Madame Bovary*, not *Emma Bovary*, and that 'Madame' tells us how aspirational and *petite bourgeoise* she is; also, the name 'Bovary' has a subliminal bovine quality to it that comments on her nature. Finally, what does the name 'Lolita' tell us? Linguistically, it is a diminutive – just three short vowels that trill easily off the tongue. It is so simple that it could probably be recognised and uttered in any language. It also has a childlike, nursery rhyme quality to it, which, of course, is perfectly in keeping with the book's themes.

Another ploy is to describe, without mentioning a character by name, a character's home in such detail that we can gauge what kind of person lives there and what they do for a living. A variation of this approach would be to put a character into a landscape (a man in a rowing boat, fishing on a lake, for example) and write a two-page character sketch using the landscape and weather to intensify the reader's sense of what kind of person that character is. When carrying out exercises like this, however, bear in mind that it is important to restrict these details of characterisation as much as possible, since it is the truth of the character we are interested in, not the facts, and, as we will see, there is a world of difference between 'character' and 'characterisation'.

'Inside out'

> 'Artists are people who are not at all interested in the facts – only in the truth. You get facts from outside. The truth you get from inside.'
>
> URSULA LE GUIN

These ruses and ploys are a good place to start for a new writer, but they can soon seem mechanical and artificial. At some point, sooner or later, you are going to have to face up to the fact that, as a writer, it is absolutely vital that you know your characters in a way that goes beyond the circumstances of their day-to-day life, beyond their 'characterisation'. It is a mistake to think that a means of paying the rent is an expression of the character's identity. However often you stick a moustache on a character, no amount of character description can reach deep down into their innermost thoughts and feelings, to their very core, their quintessence.

In the best of writing, it never takes much to summon and show a character's inner life – a brushstroke or two, nothing more. In Proust's *À la recherche du temps perdu*, for example, there is a famous moment when the narrator dips a madeleine into his cup of tea, an action that precipitates an instance of 'involuntary memory', a point in time when the narrator's past and present merge in his mind to produce a transcendental moment of epiphany and understanding about life, a nostalgic perfection, a unique sensory experience that had hitherto been unavailable to him and that he will never feel again. Although the impression is abstract and difficult to comprehend for the narrator, 'involuntary memory' is never brought on by anything other than the solid world of objects, it never recalls the indefinite article as abstraction does, and so its images are always concrete.

In his book *Speak, Memory*, Nabokov talks about a moment as a young child when he was playing a game of matchsticks with a relative who was a soldier. He remembered the matches jumping in the air when the soldier got up from the sofa. That small, seemingly unimportant detail is what brings the memory to life. Years later, that same relative, by then very old, asked Nabokov for a light, a piece of information that surpasses its purely descriptive purpose and makes an elegant yet precise comment on the passage of time and how the child becomes father to the man. The devil is in the details.

To create an 'organic', wholly rounded, credible character in this way, you have to start thinking from the inside out, so to speak. You have to write *through* a character, not around them, and a big part of that is looking for and locating in the book your main character's consciousness. Strange though it may sound, I believe that all books and their characters yet to be written already exist inside one's self, in a preverbal, rhythmic, motor place in the body. The trick is to find a way of 'tapping' into it, to find the right consciousness in the book from which to tell the story. It is rather like tuning a radio in order to find the right frequency.

You have to think beyond the page, as it were, and look inside yourself. At some point, for a character to ring true, you will have to draw on your own inner being, the part you normally keep hidden and out of reach. Ironically, if you want to express yourself, you have to give yourself away. If a moment from your life is needed for your story, then hand it over. Good characters are sympathetic subjects and dubious objects. Let them emerge gradually in the back of your mind, using your own experiences to help shape and form them.

If a moment from your life is needed for your story, then hand it over

'*Everything is copy.*'

NORA EPHRON

Draw on your experiences with those around you, too. Graham Greene talked about the necessity of having a 'splinter of ice' in the heart of a writer. If your book is going to have emotional honesty and veracity, you need to be willing to open and read other people's mail. But, even drawing on those around you, you will find that no fictional character is ever based on a single person – they are always composites. Basing a character on the personality traits of several people helps to create the illusion of a singular being but, no matter how separate these creations may feel to you, they will have your emotional fingerprints all over them. One way or another, actual biographical and autobiographical material will merge, to the point where what is real and what is invented become indistinguishable. Of your book, you can now say, 'None of this happened and it's all true.'

'*None of this happened and it's all true*'

'Acting is doing'

'The purpose of living is an end, which is a kind of activity, not a quality.'

ARISTOTLE

Aristotle's idea here is the fundamental rubric of character, the most primal, original, essential question for a writer – what are your characters going to *do*? Aristotle called action *praxis*, from which we get the word 'practical'. Think about someone you know who always talks about travelling to Marrakech, or building a shed, or learning Japanese, but has never got round to it; now compare how you feel about someone who does not just talk the talk but who actually gets on with it and does it. It is so much more impressive to see someone do what they say they will. As far as writing is concerned, the same applies – what your characters do in your story is far more revealing than what they say.

In an essay entitled 'Acting Is Doing', Sydney Pollack talks about how he directs actors. He says, 'the biggest mistake that's made in directing [actors] is talking about and working towards results instead of causes'. He goes on to say that, if he tells an actor to play a suspicious man, the actor will look for ways of playing 'suspicious'; if, however, he tells the actor to watch the other man's hand because he has a gun in his pocket, then that gives the

'Character' is dynamic, active – a verb

actor something very specific to do. 'Characterisation' is adjectival, descriptive, passive; whereas 'character' is dynamic, active – a verb.

To paraphrase Aristotle, there is really no such thing as character, other than habitual action. The very fact of a character's existence precedes their essence. Watching people do things cuts to the quick of who they are much more quickly than any amount of words. And if there is no need for a character to do anything, leave them alone until they are needed. As a character, all they can do is be as patient and as empty as possible. If characters become self-conscious, there is often an unattractive heaviness in the text, a kind of 'gravity' that burdens it, whereas what you are looking for is a kind of 'grace'. In the story, it is not what happens to them that is important, but how they react to it. A character's true fight within themselves is against this gravity, and the instrument of this fight is the idea of work, a project, a task. 'What are you *doing*?' Pollack writes. 'Acting is *doing*. Doing. Doing.'

Desire and identification

> 'We and the heroes and heroines of fiction never know
> whether obstacles create desire, or desire creates
> obstacles.'
>
> ADAM PHILLIPS

'Motivation' is an overused, jargony word, but it is true that characters have to do things for a reason. What do they want? The boy? The girl? The whale? Desire is wanting to have something, and wanting it badly. All character motivation stems from the difference between what a character has and what they want. Your job is to put obstacles in their path in order to make it difficult for them to achieve their goals – not impossible, just difficult. If a character brings about their success as a result of their own efforts in the face of great adversity, the reader will feel that success far more keenly than if it 'just happens' to come their way. The difference between what a character has and what they want is the basis for conflict and, as we will see later on, there is no story without conflict.

If desire is wanting to have something, then identification is wanting to be like someone. Such identification is the prime motivating factor in many psychological novels, or novels that delve deeply into human behaviour. A psychoanalytic theory called Object Relations states that psychological well-being is, for the most part, a matter of developing a capacity for healthy mental 'representations', which is important because it allows the person to mark out boundaries between self and the world. Neurotic representation, however, erects excessive representational boundaries between self and the world, ones that are designed to protect a vulnerable self. Such mental representations replace the actual world with private representations that are exaggeratedly developed and highly articulated, but which have no bearing on reality.

Ian McEwan's novel *Enduring Love* is just such a 'neurotic representation'. The opening, a *tour de force* of suspense (one of McEwan's signatures), involves a dramatic and tragic ballooning accident in which one man dies. Present at the accident is Joe Rose and a bystander, Jed Parry. Joe and Jed exchange looks. Unknown to Joe, though, is the fact that Jed suffers from de Clérambault's syndrome, an obsessive disorder that causes the sufferer to believe mistakenly that someone else is in love with them. Delusional and dangerous, Jed gradually wreaks havoc in Joe's life, testing the limits of his reason and driving him to the brink of murder and madness. In your own novel, ask yourself: who does my character think they are? Who do they want to be?

Choice and change

> *'Character is that which reveals personal choice, the kinds of things a man chooses or rejects when that is not obvious.'*

ARISTOTLE

If the origin of action is a character's desire put into practice, then it follows that the decisions a character makes regarding what they do (or do not do) reveal the most about their character. Self-knowledge is not only about knowing who you are, it is also about making good choices for yourself. If you make the same mistakes when faced with the same dilemma, you have not learned from the experience and you have not changed. Good judgement comes from experience, but experience comes from poor judgement. Aristotle's term for character was *ethos*, meaning 'persuasive appeal' and from which we get the word 'ethical'.

One of your jobs as a writer is to send your characters out into a story where you can shower them with circumstance, events and predicaments to see what happens, but it is only by forcing characters into difficult situations that you will see their true colours. Character is most revealed when the going gets tough. This is what Hemingway meant when he defined the 'courage' he saw in wartime as 'grace under pressure'.

As we have discussed, good character building centres on 'doing', not 'being' – on activity, not passivity – but a character can reveal themselves just as much by what they choose not to do. Self-knowledge is about making the right decisions at the right time, but it is also the case that, even though we have all the facts in front of us and know what we should do, we sometimes do not make a choice at all. Freud talked a great deal about this propensity for refusal, or denial. He wrote that when a person abolishes something internally, it will always return from the outside in the form of a delusion. The more we run away from something, the more we run into it.

In Victor Hugo's novel *Les Misérables*, for example, the policeman Javert has an obsessive desire to imprison Valjean, even though Valjean is, by the time Javert meets him, a reformed convict. For most of the novel, Javert relentlessly hunts and tracks Valjean down, only to let him slip through his fingers. Years later, during the Paris uprising of 1832, Valjean saves Javert's life, but Javert cannot cope with the mercy shown to him by Valjean and throws himself into the Seine. Despite Valjean's most profound efforts to better himself and contribute to society, he is continually hounded and persecuted by Javert. At the key dramatic moment, despite having every reason in the world to see him die, Valjean shows Javert the clemency that Javert has always denied Valjean, who actually deserves it much more. The illusion of occupying the moral high ground was, in reality, a delusion, and this realisation is what forces Javert to hurl himself into the river.

Hugo found inspiration for his novel in the story of real-life criminal/policeman Eugène François Vidocq, and he split Vidocq's personality into the two main characters for his novel. They are two sides of the same coin, a symbiotic flow of guilt and 'justice', moral enterprise and stagnation, optimism and discrimination. Throughout the novel, Javert has many opportunities to end his extreme prejudice against Valjean, but chooses not to. As a result, his bigotry gradually transforms itself into a form of neurosis, and the moment he understands this exaggerated mental representation is the moment he dies.

> *'People don't change, they only stand more nakedly revealed.'*
>
> CHARLES OLSON

This idea of the 'exchange of guilt' is one of the most powerful transformations a character can go through. Whatever its kind, characters must undergo some degree of change for a story to have any kind of justification. This is the *sine qua non* of fiction, without which a story is not a story. Aristotle said that 'Change is giving form to matter'. By a story's end, characters should be transformed. They should have learned something about themselves that they hitherto did not know, self-knowledge that they did not possess. A narrative promises to take us through a set of screens, twisting and turning through strange lands and back out again, to the place where we began, but

Characters must undergo some degree of change

where everything is now utterly different. At the close of the narrative, we and the characters are the same people but now totally altered.

The existential vs the spiritual

> 'Making a character "alive" means: getting to the bottom of his existential problem. Which in turn means: getting to the bottom of some situations, some motifs, even some words that shape him.'
>
> MILAN KUNDERA

In his book *The Art of the Novel*, Kundera writes that a novel is, fundamentally, an 'existential enquiry', and that this enquiry is determined and driven by certain 'theme-words' for his characters. In his novel *The Unbearable Lightness of Being*, those theme-words for the character of Tereza are: body; soul; vertigo; weakness; idyll; Paradise. Kundera, the ultra-modern novelist, is the ultimate puppeteer, introducing his characters like acquaintances and using them as mouthpieces for various philosophical ideas. He cannot get close to his characters; he says almost nothing about their physical appearance and there is no internal monologue in any of his novels. By maintaining this distance between himself and his characters, Kundera gives himself room enough to explore his own 'felt' subjectivity in the here-and-now. 'The novelist,' he says, 'is neither historian nor prophet: he is an explorer of existence.'

After assigning his characters these very specific traits (indeed, you could argue that Kundera's characters are nothing *but* collections of character traits), Kundera uses them repeatedly, so much so that his characters become what James Wood refers to as a 'mnemonic leitmotif'. The more complex you wish to make a character, the larger their collection of varying traits. However, be wary of this approach. Kundera may treat his characters as marionettes and mouthpieces for his ideas, but he is also a master storyteller and an intellectual powerhouse. You can reduce characters to traits, but the most memorable fictional characters have a spark of vitality in them that cannot be accounted for by any number of mnemonic leitmotifs and theme-words, and that spark cannot ultimately come from anyone except the writer.

'No man's wisdom goes beyond his experience.'
LEO TOLSTOY

One of the hardest tasks in writing characters is writing about them when they are on their own. Characters have a physical aspect in a novel, interacting with other people and the world, but what are they like when they are sitting on their own in a room? What happens when nothing happens?

Tolstoy alluded to this in his suggestion that there are two possible ways forward in life, from which people must choose. In his proposition, he says that one of these courses of action consists of giving a person a 'map' and pointing out the landmarks by which they must navigate their way. The success of finding their correct path depends entirely on the landscape, or the physical world, around them. The other method consists simply in giving the person a reading on a spiritual 'compass'. If the person keeps to this reading as they travel, not deviating in the slightest, they should find that they have stayed on the correct path.

The first type of path Tolstoy proposes makes use of external precepts, or rules: the person is given the lie of the land and they must move through the world in relation to what is around them. The second type relies more on an inner fortitude: the person is given a reading, a moral guidance, that they must take to heart and have faith in. If they keep to their word, they will inevitably reach their destination, despite whatever landmarks they may encounter along the way. This spiritual aspect is what characters can best show when they are sitting alone in a room, in touch with their inner self. Those moments when they think they are least observed by the world around them are the moments when they can reveal their innermost being. In Tolstoy's *Anna Karenina*, the character of Levin, who is in constant dialogue with himself throughout the novel regarding how best to live one's life, is generally acknowledged as a self-portrait of Tolstoy himself.

Deep interiority

> 'Respect your characters, even the minor ones. In art,
> as in life, everyone is the hero of their own particular
> story.'
>
> SARAH WATERS

In Knut Hamsun's Modernist novel *Hunger*, the starving main character (who remains nameless) wanders the streets of Oslo, encountering various strangers from whom he tries to scrounge a meal. His 'hunger' is not just for nourishment, however – he is drawn to make contact with the people he meets, but he also rejects them as soon as they show signs of responding to his requests. He craves, but ultimately cannot accept, help from his fellow man. In an article on the book, James Wood describes the character as an 'epistemological brawler', blaming his fate on God and vowing not to succumb to any sense he has of the divine world order. His mental representation of the world becomes increasingly unstable as his grip on reality loosens and paranoia sets in. Taken by themselves, his thought processes are perfectly logical, yet his mental and physical states deteriorate to an alarming degree and he is eventually forced to quit the city.

In the text, his character is represented not as a continuous 'wave', but as a storm of interruptions. Hamsun, like Chekhov, was deeply suspicious of novels that presented characters as smooth and well rounded, without flaws or foibles, lacking the angst he felt was the natural response to the brutal realities of modern life. Later, Virginia Woolf reacted in much the same way, stating that, for Edwardian novelists like Arnold Bennett, character was purely everything that could be described – houses, clothes, polite conversation. Woolf, however, felt passionately that character was everything that could *not* be described.

The attempt to show the life of the mind was the aim of many Modernists, including Hamsun, Chekhov, Woolf, Joyce and Henry James, who described this deep interiority as 'an immense sensibility, a kind of huge spider-web of the finest silken threads suspended in the chamber of consciousness, catching every air-borne particle in its tissue'.

One of our duties as writers is to acknowledge and explore the complexity of human life and experience, rather than merely subject characters to overdisciplined and organised plots. Genre fiction might help us get through the day, but perhaps not our lives, and the idea of deep interiority is usually at odds with the demands of pure plot. Furthermore, it is the case that, since the Second World War, the Postmodern experiment has produced books that are much more concerned with connectivity and contingency than with depth of character.

Point of view
The place from which we 'see' the story, the perceptual vantage point

The 'narrator' is what we call the person through whom we see the story, although they need not be a character in the story: they are an agent adopted by the author to be the fictitious spokesperson in the text. Point of view is all about the narrator's distance and focus. Are you going to get up close and personal to a character? Or will you 'shoot' everything in mid or long shot? Who is the centre of your story, and is the person you are going to focus on the same as your narrator? Deciding through whom we are going to see the story, and from where, is one of the most crucial decisions you will make as a writer.

'Suture'

Whatever the answers to these questions, 'suture' is the way in which *any* point of view is established. 'Suture' refers to the manner in which we are stitched into the fictional world, or 'fabric', of a narrative. The process ensures that we are 'drawn into' the fictional world, taking up positions as 'subjects-within-the-text'. The most common way we are situated into a text is by suturing us into a position of identification with a particular character. In narrative cinema and fiction, this is achieved by shot/reverse shot patterning, which shows us an image and then assigns the viewing of that image to a particular character in the text, thus ensuring identification with them.

Often, however, we may be sutured into the text to identify with the observer of the story, a character who is inside the fictional space but not part of the action. Nick Carraway in F. Scott Fitzgerald's *The Great Gatsby*, for instance, is the narrator of the story, but he is not a contributor to the plot; he is just the observer, the medium through which we see the story unfold. Because we are aligned with Carraway's point of view, we, too, are subjects-within-the-text and share his role as 'sleeping partner' in the text. It is interesting to note how surreptitious and effective this process is, rather like the narrative process itself – we hardly notice the 'seams' at all when a text is successfully suturing us into its fabric without our knowledge or consent.

When deciding on your point of view, you have five options to choose from: first person, second person (very rare indeed), single or multiple third person, and an omniscient point of view. The points of view, from third-person singular and multiple through to the omniscient, comprise a kind of sliding scale, rather than a series of disjunctions, as the focus of the story is diffused from one person to many, and ultimately to an all-knowing, all-seeing entity in the sky.

First person

First-person point of view uses the pronoun 'I'. All the action is seen through the eyes of one person to whom we stay in close proximity throughout the story, looking over their shoulder, as it were, as events unfold before our eyes (although it is important to note that the 'I' telling the story need not be telling their *own* story). This means that we see and hear only what the narrator can see and hear – our perspective is restricted and the action can never be opened out beyond this viewpoint. However, whatever perspective we might lose with a first-person viewpoint is more than compensated for by what we gain in intimacy. First-person narration is particularly suited to character studies and 'confessional' narratives.

Whatever perspective we might lose with a first-person viewpoint is more than compensated for by what we gain in intimacy

J. D. Salinger's *Catcher in the Rye* and Sylvia Plath's *The Bell Jar* are both examples of confessional narratives, both written in the first person. Just think how different they would be in the third person – all their colour, flavour and depth of character would be lost. Writing his book in the first person allowed Salinger to climb into the mind of Holden Caulfield and conflate his voice with his viewpoint, so that we not only see what he sees, but we hear what he has to say about it. The greatest pleasure in Salinger's book is the voice of Caulfield, a voice rendered with complete sympathy and authenticity.

William Faulkner's novel *As I Lay Dying* is as an example of that rare thing – a novel written from multiple first-person viewpoints. Not only that, but each narrator's story is represented as stream-of-consciousness, occasionally making no concessions at all to standard speech or grammar. Although Faulkner helps us through this potential minefield by naming each new narrator as they take up the narrative baton, so to speak, voice is even more essential here – apart from names, it is the only thing that differentiates between the series of 'I's, but the book is so skilfully written that we soon learn to distinguish between the fifteen different narrators. Graham Swift used a similar structure in his novel *Last Orders*.

This use of multiple first-person narrators is also employed by Orhan Pamuk in his murder mystery *My Name Is Red*, set in Turkey in the 1590s, among the world of the Sultan's miniaturists and illustrators. Here, Pamuk uses twenty different narrators, ten of which are the disembodied 'voices' of the colours in the exquisite illuminations painted by the leading characters – hence the title *My Name Is Red*. Nine of the narrators are the illustrators themselves, of which the murderer is one. The final narrator is the voice of the murdered man himself, bitterly recounting his tale of woe and imploring anyone who may be listening to avenge his death.

Indeed, first-person point of view has a long tradition in murder mysteries in particular, and crime fiction in general, starting with Wilkie Collins' *The Moonstone*, which is written as a series of first-person testimonies and is generally considered to be the first detective novel published in the UK. With its publication, *The Moonstone* introduced a number of elements that were to become staples of the classic detective story: the 'locked room' mystery in an English country house; the 'inside job'; red herrings; a celebrated and skilful professional investigator (the wonderful Sergeant Cuff); a large number of suspects; a reconstruction of the crime; and a final twist in the plot.

In the text, the detective is there *in praesentia* for the reader, and so the reader can only know what the detective knows. We go over the same ground as the criminal (and the author), picking up clues and following the trail. If the investigator follows a red herring and makes a wrong turn in their case, so do we. First-person narration can be a very effective conjuring act, making it easy for the author to spring surprises on the detective (and us) and keep suspense levels high.

In Agatha Christie's *The Murder of Roger Ackroyd*, for example, we see events unfold through the eyes of the village doctor, Dr Sheppard, as he helps Hercule Poirot to investigate the murder of the eponymous victim. There are several plausible suspects but, in the end, Poirot reveals the murderer as the doctor himself. It is an odd, unsettling moment when Poirot points the finger at him and, by default, at us, too. This powerful, shocking ending forces us to re-evaluate everything the doctor has told us, and we begin to see the details he has omitted and the gaps in time when he must have been 'abroad', committing the crimes. It is a wonderful example of the ultimate confidence trick – we feel simultaneously collared and hoodwinked.

The unreliable narrator

'Tell the truth but tell it slant.'

EMILY DICKINSON

First-person perspective is ideal for creating such unreliable narrators. The first-person narrators in these kinds of texts are usually talking to themselves, or to the readers, just as much as they are telling a story. Unreliable narrators are economical with the truth because they are in denial about some aspect of themselves or because they have something to hide. They force us to see through eyes that sharpen, shade, slant or skewer reality. When reading texts narrated by characters we cannot trust, we have to learn to read between the lines to seek the truth; we have to cast ourselves as detectives, picking up meaning 'behind' the narrator's account and putting together the real version of events for ourselves.

Unreliable narrators are economical with the truth because they are in denial about some aspect of themselves

Kazuo Ishiguro has talked of his use of the 'unreliable narrator' – the literary trope for which he is perhaps best known. The point he made was that unreliable narrators are often a result of people reassessing their lives and the disappointment of it and, if the feeling of disappointment was too great, narrators might choose to leaven it in order to make it manageable. He went on to say that he auditions all his characters before deciding which one to offer the role of narrator to. Imagine the Sherlock Holmes stories with Holmes himself as the narrator, he said – they would just not have worked. The point of the Holmes stories is that we are in the same boat as Watson with regard to the amount of information we have. Like Watson, we are in the dark most of the time. With regard to Ishiguro's own work, think of *The Remains of the Day* and how different it would have been had Miss Kenton narrated the story. Her self-awareness and emotional articulacy, which Stevens so obviously lacks, would have meant that the pleasure of the text would have to have come from some other place entirely. So, adopting different characters as narrators produces different kinds of books.

This is also the case with Humbert Humbert, the narrator in Nabokov's *Lolita*. During the course of the narrative, Humbert Humbert repeatedly tries to make light of his 'predilection' and aims to paint as rosy a picture as possible of his road trip and eventual settlement with twelve-year-old Dolores Haze. *Lolita* has very dark subject matter at its heart, but Humbert Humbert tries to make this subject matter more palatable by the urbanity, intelligence and wit of his narration. Speaking after the fact, Humbert Humbert has distanced himself from his acts, a gap he fills with language that sparkles and shines, but flatters to deceive. He is detached from events, but he has a desire to be heard and, if not sympathised with, then at least understood. He is an *outré* outcast from society and therefore speaks from the margins. This *tour de force* narrative is a linguistic high-wire act, but is also a huge confidence trick, with Humbert Humbert continually attempting to pull the wool over our eyes.

Second person

The second-person point of view – 'you' – is rarely used in fiction; it is far more common in lyric poetry. When it is used in fiction, it creates a highly charged relationship between narrator and reader. By addressing the reader directly, the narrator makes the reader complicit. It forces them into the fictional world, whether they like it or not, thus creating a sense of danger and immediacy. But this is a very specialised point of view and hard for a reader to stay with for the length of an entire novel. Such complicity can become claustrophobic, bullying even – there is nowhere for the reader to turn, nowhere to have a breather. This relationship between narrator and reader is promoted at the expense of characters and story, and most readers will quickly tire and switch off if there is no story, so it is to be approached with caution.

Third person – single

A single third-person viewpoint can seem remarkably similar to the first-person point of view, albeit a little cooler, more distant. J. M. Coetzee's *Disgrace* is a good example of a novel that is written in the third person, but feels as though it is in the first. A large part of this effect is created by the use of the present tense, which brings an acute sense of immediacy to proceedings. Not only that, but the present tense Coetzee uses is the 'present perfect' – 'to have gone', for example. The first line is: 'For a man of his age, fifty-two, divorced, he has, to his mind, solved the problem of sex rather well.' If he had used the 'simple past' tense here ('had'), the impression would have been that the narrator had some kind of vantage point beyond the closed events of the story. Keeping to the present perfect, however, gets us into the mind of the character and tells us that the ending of the story is not yet known, that everything that happens is contingent and the outcome provisional.

In the Coetzee sentence, if you were to replace the third person with the first, the meaning of the sentence is kept, illustrating again how close first- and third-person narratives can be. But this is the exception, not the rule. If you have a sad story to tell (and Coetzee's story is very sad indeed), presenting it in third person, as opposed to first, will nearly always render it slightly less intense. As similar as first- and single third-person points of view may initially appear, however, they are not completely interchangeable. It is a mistake to think that you can simply change the first-person pronoun 'I' to the third-person pronoun 'he' or 'she' and maintain perfect narrative clarity and comprehension. Occasionally, it works, but it is usually not possible to make a simple transition from first to third person. Try it for yourself: take a passage of writing, change the point of view from first to third person as you read, or *vice versa*, and see what happens.

The narrator as stenographer, interpreter or reporter?

The narrator and main character are the same person in first-person narratives. This is, by definition, not the case with third-person narratives. In spite of that, however, it is still possible to align narrator and character extremely close together, and the degree to which the narrator aligns themselves with the character is set as a kind of sliding scale, ranging from remaining steadfastly outside the character's body to purposefully climbing inside their head and heart.

The degree to which the narrator aligns themselves with the character is set as a kind of sliding scale

As with a court stenographer, one role the narrator can play is to act as nothing more than a medium through which we see directly for ourselves what the characters do and say. In this role, the narrator makes no attempt to tell us what the characters are thinking or feeling; the narration is merely a transcription. It is all about action and words, not moods or emotions. The important point here is that the narrator remains so 'invisible' in the text that the story seems as though it is being shown to us first-hand, as it were – directly, without mediation.

There are certain kinds of writing that lend themselves particularly well to the role of narrator-as-stenographer.

The 'hardboiled' crime stories written by Dashiell Hammett, for example, are stripped down to their bare bones of action and direct speech. The narrator in Hemingway's early fiction, too, is nowhere to be seen.

'Free indirect style'

Further along the scale lies the moment when the narrator enters the body, and the view from which the story is told shifts to a point somewhere inside the character. Now, the narrator is not so preoccupied with showing us what a character says and does as they are with relaying to us what the character is thinking and feeling. This role allows the narrator to 'listen in' on what the character is thinking and feeling, rather like an interpreter in a booth with headphones on relaying to us someone's thoughts as faithfully as possible.

But how can we enter the heart and mind of a character when we are in the third person? Well, there is 'interior monologue', where the narrator tries to record a character's thoughts for an extended period. But huge chunks of interior monologue can feel clunky and might turn the reader off. There is a much more subtle technique that can do this, a technique called 'free indirect style', which is one of fiction's best-kept secrets.

The sentence '"I will stay here tomorrow," she thought' is an example of 'direct speech', a report of which would be: 'She thought that she would stay the next day.' Technically speaking, free indirect style takes the past tense and third person of reported speech – 'she would stay' – and combines them with the time and place of direct speech – 'here tomorrow' – to come up with: 'She would stay here tomorrow.' It is called 'free' because it has no tags ('she thought', 'he said') and 'indirect' because it is reported speech.

Put simply, this writing style can be summed up as a fusion of third-person point of view with first-person consciousness, a way of bridging the two and bringing characters to life when writing in third person. It is a miraculous device because, although it is still technically a form of reported speech, it is very much the case that it sounds more like a character 'speaking' than a narrator 'reporting'. (Be warned, though, that free indirect style works best only when used sparingly – if you stay in the mind of the character for an extended period, it becomes internal monologue.)

A *fusion of third-person point of view with first-person consciousness*

But how do you know if you are using it correctly? The litmus test to see if it is being used properly is to say aloud to yourself the moment you think is free indirect style. Does it sound like the kind of thing someone would naturally say to themselves? If the answer is yes, then it is free indirect style. If the answer is no, then it is because you are still relying on the narrator to tell us a character's thoughts. Free indirect style is all about allowing us to hear *directly* what characters are thinking to themselves and so needs to sound natural – the more colloquial it is, the more natural it will sound.

Like all the best tools and techniques of fiction, a lot of writers will already be using free indirect style without realising it as it has been around for ages. Flaubert, writing in the nineteenth century, was one of its great exponents. Here is an example from *Madame Bovary*:

> She looked about her with the wish that the earth might crumble about her. Why not end it all? What restrained her? She was free. She advanced, looking at the paving stones, saying to herself, 'Come! come!'

Each moment of free indirect style – 'Why not end it all? What restrained her? She was free' – is a 'dip' into Emma's consciousness, a dip that captures only fleetingly what she is thinking to herself. Little dips like these dotted here and there bring a freshness and vitality to a character much more successfully than any amount of internal monologue.

'Stream-of-consciousness'

Despite being an attempt at capturing the complexity of deep interiority, these forms – interior monologue and free indirect style – still respect and preserve the standard grammatical and syntactical conventions of the language. 'Stream-of-consciousness', however, does not. As it implies, the term (coined by Henry James' psychologist brother, William) refers to the attempt by the narrator not only to capture the product of the thought process, but to capture the process of thought itself. Stream-of-consciousness goes a step further into consciousness, in that it encapsulates not only cognitive processes, but also perceptions.

Seymour Chatman uses the example that whereas it is perfectly normal to say to yourself 'I must get milk and bread' while walking along a path, it is rare to say 'That rose is red' when you pass a garden. The former is a verbalised thought, whereas the latter is something perceived. 'The latter,' Chatman says, 'is something "felt" rather than said.' As well as verbalised thought processes, it is exactly these perceptions that stream-of-consciousness also attempts to capture. In stream-of-consciousness, the narrator is so deeply embedded within the character that they are not there; their presence goes unnoticed. Stream-of-consciousness narrative is body language, but without the body. This is when a narrator is most like an interpreter – headphones on, locked into a character's head, repeating what they hear as faithfully as they can. Virginia Woolf and James Joyce were both famous exponents of this technique.

Stream-of-consciousness narrative is body language, but without the body

'Telling'

All the aforementioned roles that a narrator can play – narrator-as-stenographer, showing us seemingly invisibly what a character says and does, and narrator-as-interpreter of what a character thinks and feels by means of free indirect style and stream-of-consciousness – allow characters to shine through unmediated. In these roles, narrators choose not to offer their own commentary or value-judgement on what a character says, does, thinks or feels.

There are moments, however, when the narrator separates themselves from these roles and chooses to offer their personal opinion. The narrator is now 'telling' us, seemingly for our benefit, the real meaning or significance of those words, actions, thoughts or feelings. This is the instance when the narrator's role in the telling of the story is at its most obviously visible in the narrative. These comments have little to do with story, adding instead an extra layer of narration.

This tendency of the narrator is what is at stake in the old saying 'Show, don't tell'. This maxim, attributed to Henry James, refers to the role assigned to a narrator whereby they interject and comment on events, confirming to us what we have already seen for ourselves, or interrupting to announce what we are about to see for ourselves. These interjections usually use the verbs 'to be' and 'to feel' to describe states of being. For example: 'She felt sad' or 'Her grief was boundless' or 'She was beside herself with excitement'. The temptation for new writers is to try to 'bolster' a moment with such interjections, to imbue it with portent, but rather than empowering the moment, this tendency impoverishes it. It will be a much more powerful experience for the reader if they feel this sadness, grief or excitement for themselves, not have the narrator tell us that it is so. We need to see these things first-hand, not hear about them second-hand from a third party.

'Show, don't tell' means writing about what is visible and tangible in order to speak of what is invisible and intangible. If you rely on the narrator to tell us what the character is feeling or thinking, we have no choice but to take it on trust and we are kept at arm's length from the characters and the story. Remove the narrator from the process of telling your story, however, and now the story unfolds naturally in the mind of the reader, drawing them in as they watch and listen to the words and actions of the characters and working out for themselves what it all means. So, for example, instead of writing 'She felt sad', you could write something like:

'Show, don't tell' means writing about what is visible and tangible in order to speak of what is invisible and intangible

A woman goes for a walk at dusk down to a very large lake. She walks along the shore, picking her way carefully over the bigger rocks. Across the expanse of water, she hears a single curlew note, which hangs in the dusk. She cannot see the bird. She remembers the morning down here when she and her son found a dead curlew. It looked like a scrap of material. It has been four months since she last saw her son. It grows darker. She keeps looking for the bird before realising that she will not see it. Unable to walk any further, she sits on a boulder and looks across the dark, flat water. She can't see the other side. Some minutes pass and then she cries quietly to herself.

Of course, 'telling' *per se* is not 'wrong'. Characters who are also first-person narrators, often in a very unreliable way, are 'telling' their own stories, but we sense in *The Remains of the Day* and *Lolita* that Ishiguro and Nabokov have deliberately chosen to let their narrators do so. Crucially, we sense the author's *intention*. 'Telling' that feels 'wrong' only happens when a writer is not sure enough of their story, or when they lack confidence to tackle a crucial scene. At such moments, 'telling' seems good enough to a new writer, but it is actually a lazy, easy option and is usually just a 'note to self'. 'Telling' happens when writers become 'blind' to their writing selves. Of course, there is no right or wrong way to do anything in a novel, but, when the reader senses that the author is showing intention in everything they do, they will feel they are in a safe pair of hands and will be willing to accept and go along with any kind of role you assign to your narrator.

Third person – multiple

The clearest advantage of a multiple third-person viewpoint is that the narrator can move into the hearts and minds of more than one character, thus opening out the story considerably. What we gain in perspective with this point of view, however, we lose in intimacy. Because of this increase in perspective, this kind of viewpoint is particularly (but not

What we gain in perspective with this point of view, however, we lose in intimacy

exclusively) suited to writing that needs an impersonal, broad canvas on which to work. Establishing shots and wide-angle viewpoints – these are devices typical of more plot-driven stories, such as thrillers, epics and historical narratives. Scenes are rendered much more 'flatly', in long shot, so that the action may unfold without narratorial comment. If an intimate first-person narrative is written in a minor key, a multiple third-person epic is all crashing major chords.

Thrillers using this panoramic point of view can flit between characters and locations, showing us how they all connect in their own way to the central story and to each other. This can generate a great deal of suspense because we know, even if they do not, what is likely to happen to certain characters. Richard Price's *Freedomland* and Courttia Newland's *Society Within* are good examples of this technique, both of which have intricate plotting set against an impressive widescreen *vérité* sweep.

The tension in this form of narrative can be made even more palpable by giving the reader/viewer more information than any of the characters. This kind of viewpoint is called 'dramatic irony' and is the kind of suspense on which Hitchcock built his entire career. In his film *Sabotage* (based on Joseph Conrad's *The Secret Agent*), for example, a boy sits on a bus playing with a puppy. Unbeknownst to him, there is a ticking bomb in the film canister he is supposed to be delivering. The tension mounts, we close in on some faces, laughing, talking, and then – *kaboom!*

We know what is going to happen but, unable to communicate this information to the character, we cannot bear the anticipation. When *Sabotage* was released, there was public outrage at a puppy being killed – they did not seem to mind about the boy and everyone else on the bus. So skilful is Hitchcock in building this kind of tension that most people do not realise just how heavily (but surreptitiously) they are being manipulated.

Omniscient

> 'The author in his book must be like God in the
> universe: everywhere present and nowhere visible.'
>
> GUSTAVE FLAUBERT

The omniscient viewpoint is the classic, God-like view of the world beloved of nineteenth-century novelists. All-seeing and all-knowing, the narrator is free and unfettered, able to range over huge distances and penetrate people's hearts and minds. The narrator here acts as a highly polished mirror, reflecting everything it sees. This point of view has fallen out of fashion and is not used so much these days, though it can be used to dramatic effect. In Cormac McCarthy's novel *The Crossing*, there is a moment when the narrator cuts from the close-up of a horse's eye to the sun rising over an enormous stretch of desert. The sudden switch from extreme close-up to furthest long shot is exhilarating.

Versions of the truth

Point of view can be used to show how different perspectives on the same set of events do not always corroborate each other. Akira Kurosawa's film *Rashomon* was the first Japanese film to be seen in the West and, in 1951, won the Golden Lion at the Venice Film Festival. Beautifully shot and edited, it is the story of the murder of a samurai warrior and the rape of his wife. The murder in the woods is witnessed by a woodcutter and a bandit is arrested for the crime. What follows is a series of four testimonies, each conflicting with the others as the characters manipulate their own actions into appearing less blameworthy than they actually were.

Rashomon is a good example of *kishōtenketsu*, a four-panel story structure that originated in Chinese poetry and is commonly used in Japanese storytelling, especially in manga comics (and in Western comic strips such as *Peanuts* and *Calvin and Hobbes*). There are four acts: *ki* is the introduction, which establishes the characters and situation. This is followed by *shō*, the development section (the original Chinese means to continue or carry forward). The third act, called *ten*, is the heart of the narrative and presents some form of twist, change of perspective or disconnection from the first two acts. The conclusion is called *ketsu* (meaning to unite, join or connect) and reconciles the first three acts into one complete work.

Compared to standard Western structures, *kishōtenketsu* is a very different way of thinking about storytelling. There is usually no definitive ending but rather an ambiguity that leaves readers/viewers to make up their own minds about what the story might mean and where it might lead the characters in future, which is exactly the case in *Rashomon*. The point made elegantly and subtly in the film is that everyone has their own version of the truth and that none of these versions is ever the whole truth. We never discover what really happened because each witness to the murder paints their own involvement in it in the best possible light. In *Rashomon*, the term 'point of view' has a double meaning: it refers to a character's perceptual vantage point, but also to their opinion. Thus, the inherent semantic link between these two meanings of the term is made explicit and the text takes on a profound degree of ambiguity.

'Voice'

Many new writers are told that one of the most vital things for a writer to do is 'find your voice', as if you had once lost it. Without your innate 'voice', they say, you are indistinct as a writer, you have no signature. 'Finding your voice' is one of the biggest myths in writing and has caused more loss of heart for new writers than anything else. You can no more 'find' your voice than you can relax when told to. Telling someone to relax is the thing least likely to make them do so.

Rather, when new writers are told that they have to find their 'voice', what they are, in fact, being told is that it may take some time before they grow sufficiently in confidence to let whatever inherent ability they may have shine through in their books. What we mean when we say a writer has found their 'voice' is that their storytelling abilities and prose style have reached some kind of zenith in textual terms. The 'implied author' in their texts is some kind of version of their writing 'voice'.

In narratological terms, what this term is actually referring to is the tone of voice the narrator speaks in, the quality of language in their report. It refers to the speech patterns, 'marker' phrases, linguistic tics and idiosyncrasies used by the author to reveal the personality of the narrator. So, while 'voice' may refer to the author's fluency of expression, or writing style, here it is used to talk about how the narrator *sounds*.

A caution from the outset: although they are inextricably entwined, 'voice' is *not* the same thing as point of view and the two terms should not be used interchangeably. Point of view is the perceptual vantage point from which the story is told, it is about what you *see*; 'voice', on the other hand, is about what you *hear*. The crucial point to remember is that perspective and expression do not necessarily come from the same person. As with the difference between 'story' and 'plot', this is an issue that causes great confusion and frustration for new writers, so let us look at it in more detail.

Point of view is about what you see; 'voice' is about what you hear

In his book *Story and Discourse*, Seymour Chatman posits four comments on the same, complete event:

'I felt myself fall down the hill.'
'I saw Jack fall down the hill.'
'Mary, poor dear, saw Jack fall down the hill.'
'Jack fell down the hill.'

Looking at the one event from these four perspectives, we can say with certainty that it is Jack who fell down the hill. The 'I' in the first sentence, then, is Jack, who is narrating his own story. In the second sentence, however, he is no longer the narrator, but we do not know who is. In the third sentence, the fact that Mary is the witness to Jack's fall is reported by a third party, so this clears up who the 'I' is in the second sentence – Mary. So, Mary was present at the scene and she witnessed Jack's fall. In the second sentence, she is the narrator *and* a character in the story. In the third sentence, however, who is this third party that reported to us that Mary saw Jack fall? We do not know, but whoever it is, one thing is clear: in the third sentence, the point of view from which the story is told is assigned to a narrator who is *not* a character. Finally, in the fourth sentence, it is not clear at all who witnessed Jack's fall – the narrator is omniscient.

The aim of this example, Chatman says, is to demonstrate that 'perspective and . . . expression need not be lodged in the same person'. The narrator in the third sentence was not present at the scene, but, in reporting the event, shows some sympathy ('poor dear'). It was not necessary for the narrator to show any feeling one way or the other in reporting the fact that Mary saw Jack's fall but, in addition to reporting the facts of the case, they chose to do so. Even in this brief example, this sympathy is what reveals the narrator's personality to us – it is the narrator's 'voice'.

To illustrate this point further, Chatman goes on to quote examples from three texts:

'A few moments [later] he found himself on the stage amid the garish gas and the dim scenery.' (From James Joyce's *A Portrait of the Artist as a Young Man*)

'He shivered a little, and I beheld him rise slowly as if a steady hand from above had been pulling him out of the chair by the hair.' (From Joseph Conrad's *Lord Jim*)

'Coffin now. Got here before us, dead as he is. Horse looking round at it with his plume skewways. Dull eye: collar tight on his neck, pressing on a bloodvessel or something.' (From James Joyce's *Ulysses*)

In the first example, the perceptual vantage point is that of Stephen Dedalus, but he is not the narrator. We know this because, if Stephen were the narrator, it would sound unnatural and implausible for him to pass judgement on how the stage seemed to him (the 'garish gas and dim scenery') at precisely the moment he stepped onto it. The pejorative adjectives here are the narrator's, not Stephen's, and they bring to light the 'voice' of the narrator.

In the second example, the 'I' is a character in the text and is the point of view from which we see the story (the narrator), so the perceptions are the character's. Despite the character perceiving the action in the first instance, however, the act of reporting it ('I beheld him rise . . .') places an implicit distance between the narrator-as-witness and the narrator-as-reporter. In both cases, though, the narrator's 'voice' is not made so apparent because the narration is purely descriptive of the action – there is no narratorial 'comment'.

The final example is a little less straightforward (as things always are in *Ulysses*). The narrator here is Leopold Bloom, so we are seeing things through his eyes, but the words he uses are so interior that we are not sure who exactly is speaking. The boundary between character and narrator is blurred here because narrator and character are so closely conflated. This is typical of stream-of-consciousness narration, in which the narrator is not 'mediating' so much as 'capturing' a character's thought processes. It is not as if Bloom is thinking to himself – the words come from a deeper place than that; it is almost as though there is no narrator at all (though of course there is).

To illustrate the idea of 'voice' for yourself, there is a well-known writing exercise, suggested by John Gardner, in which the writer has to describe a barn as seen by a person whose son has just been killed in a war. The trick is that you are not allowed to mention that fact, so the writing becomes an exercise in pure 'voice' as the building becomes imbued with the narrator's mood. The writer then has to repeat the exercise, this time from the point of view of a person who is in love. But, again, you are not allowed to mention that fact. In both cases, the hidden agendas remain secret, and the barn becomes 'animated'.

To sum up: the kind of role you assign your narrator is one of the most fundamental and crucial decisions you will make when writing fiction. Are you going to allow your narrator to do no more than 'record' the words and actions of your characters? Or will you let them delve deeply into their interior life? The decisions regarding how much you allow your narrator to be involved in the telling of your story will largely determine what kind of book you write.

In any reading and writing experience, there is a complex set of relationships between the author, narrator, characters and reader. As the writer, which of these relationships do you wish to promote? If the author and narrator are 'one' with each other, you are taking the reader into the realms of autobiography or memoir. If, on the other hand, you wish to encourage a rapport between the narrator and the reader, the narrator may well address the reader directly, thus bypassing character (and therefore story) altogether. This can lead to a certain playfulness on the narrator's part, depending on how sincere the narrator wishes to be. The narrator may, for instance, not be telling the truth, and so the reader gradually learns to mistrust their version of events, or perhaps they adopt an ironic tone with respect to the story they are telling.

If, however, you want the narrator and characters to be as closely aligned as possible, your narrator has a choice of either showing us directly what the characters say and do, or entering into their hearts and minds to tell us what they feel and think. In both cases, the narrator can be a 'transparent medium', largely invisible, but they can also make their presence felt in the narrative and play a more conspicuous role in the telling of the story.

'Tell me and I'll forget. Show me and I'll remember. Involve me and I'll understand.'

CHINESE PROVERB

Dialogue
What makes good dialogue?
How can we tell?

Think of a scene you remember from a favourite book or film and the chances are that it will be memorable mainly because of its dialogue (which works in very similar ways, and on much the same level, in both fiction and film). There is nothing as fascinating or appealing to people as what they say to each other, and dialogue is the aspect of fiction or a film that can hold the reader's interest to the greatest degree. But good dialogue is one of the hardest aspects of fiction to get right. If you eavesdrop on people talking in a café or on a bus, and transcribe it, you will find it full of repetitions, slang, bad language, silences, *non sequiturs*, 'you know's', 'likes', none of which is interesting to read. One of the fundamental things to appreciate about good dialogue is that it is an *impression* of how people really speak – an approximation, not a facsimile.

Another thing to remember is to try to keep dialogue down to a minimum. The temptation for new writers is to write reams and reams of dialogue, expanding it to the point where any meaning it might have contained completely disappears, whereas what they should be doing is compressing the dialogue, keeping it down to a minimum so that meaning expands as much as possible. This requires making it quite unrealistic, but do not worry: the semantic 'leaps' between lines of dialogue can be much greater than you think. Dialogue is not 'real'; it is an intensification of speech.

Dialogue is not 'real'; it is an intensification of speech

Here are two excerpts from films. Which one do you think is an example of good dialogue and which bad? Why?

'You know, when I was a kid, I always thought I was gonna grow up to be a hero.'
'Well, it's too late now.'

'What did you expect from this?'
'I don't know – maybe some self-realisation.'

In the first exchange, from *Butch Cassidy and the Sundance Kid* (written by William Goldman), we understand that the speakers know each other well, that there is a strong enough bond between them to allow for this kind of open banter. The dialogue is attractively warm and witty. The idealism and cynicism in the lines are 'markers' for the characters of Butch and Sundance, respectively, things that differentiate between them and identify them as individuals. This rich exchange of words reveals character to us, and good dialogue should grow out of character and the story in this way.

In the second exchange (taken from *Van Helsing*), however, the connection between the speakers is not so clear and the dialogue is too 'on the nose': it is telling us something about the character instead of showing it. This makes for bad dialogue.

Think of a scene from a film you saw or a book you read recently that contained a lot of dialogue and make a list of the functions you think the dialogue performed. Then add what else you think dialogue should do. How many of the following functions did the dialogue perform? It should:

1 Characterise the speaker, and perhaps the person addressed.
2 Be idiomatic, maintaining the individuality of the speaker, yet still blend with the story.
3 Reflect the speaker's mood.
4 Reveal motivation, or attempt to hide it.
5 Show relationship of character to other characters.
6 Be connective; that is, grow out of the preceding speech and lead into the next.
7 Advance the action.
8 Carry information/exposition.
9 Foreshadow what is to come.
10 Be clear and comprehensible to the audience.

In Michael Mann's *Collateral*, Max, a Los Angeles taxi driver played by Jamie Foxx, has unknowingly picked up an assassin, Vincent, played by Tom Cruise. Vincent has hired Max for the night because he has to make several stops. At the first of these stops, Max is waiting for Vincent in an alleyway when a body falls on the roof of his cab. Max looks on aghast. Vincent returns and pulls a gun on him.

Here is an excerpt of dialogue from the film. As you read through the scene, tick off how many of the above criteria the scene fulfils.

Vincent: We gotta make the best of it, improvise . . . Darwin, shit happens, I-Ching, whatever – we gotta roll with it.

Max: I-Ching? What you talking about, man? You threw a man out a window!

Vincent: I didn't throw him. He fell.

Max: But what did he do to you?

Vincent: Nothing. I only met him tonight.

Max: You just met him once and you kill him like that?

Vincent: What, I should only kill people after I get to know them?

Max: No, man . . .

Vincent: Max, six billion people on the planet . . . You're getting bent out of shape over one fat guy?

Max: Well, who was he?

Vincent: What do you care? Have you ever heard of Rwanda?

Max: Yes, I know Rwanda.

Vincent: Tens of thousands killed before sundown. Nobody's killed people that fast since Nagasaki and Hiroshima. Did you bat an eye, Max? Did you join Amnesty International, Oxfam, Save the Whale, Greenpeace or something?

Max: No.

Vincent: But I off one fat Angeleno and you throw a hissy fit.

How many of the functions did you tick? In the scene, Vincent and Max are obviously at odds with each other (5); Max is horrified and Vincent is aggressive (3); Vincent is shown to be purposeful, yet can adapt to changing situations (1); the words 'Darwin, shit happens, I-Ching, whatever' are an idiomatic 'marker' of Vincent's personality (2); the plot – that Vincent forces Max to drive him around LA during the course of one night – is advanced (7). In addition, the dialogue carries a certain amount of information, it foreshadows what is to come, it is connective, and is clear and comprehensible to the audience. The only function it does not perform is number 4, because Max does not yet know that Vincent is an assassin, a fact that Vincent goes to great lengths to keep from him.

This passage is an excellent illustration of how many things good dialogue can do at any one time. Dialogue should not only snap, crackle and pop on the page but it should also perform as many of these functions as possible *at the same time*.

Subtext

When writing dialogue, always be thinking about the subtext of what characters say, the meaning behind their words. There is a great scene in Woody Allen's *Annie Hall* when Annie (played by Diane Keaton) and Alvy (played by Allen himself) are both in therapy and the true meaning of what they say pops up on screen as subtitles. This could be done easily in a novel by having a character say a line of dialogue and have a thought that contradict each other. Making characters simply say what they mean will usually lead to flat and dull dialogue, but putting a façade on a character, so that we have to dig behind what they say to find out what they really mean, is far more intriguing and involving for the reader.

Not only can characters not mean what they say, they might not actually be listening to another person at all. In life, people often do not really listen to their friend, lover or relative, because they are too busy thinking about what they want to say and are merely waiting for the opportunity to do so. In such situations, there is not really a 'dialogue' going on – at moments like this, dialogue is more like two monologues that only sometimes connect. Having your characters talk 'evenly' back and forth to each other, like a game of ping pong, can lead to dreary and two-dimensional dialogue,

Dialogue is more like two monologues that only sometimes connect

while having them talking 'at odds' like this, addressing their own issues instead of the other person's, is an effective way of revealing character and showing the conflict within and between them.

Story vs plot
Putting one time scheme inside another

> 'A writer is someone who can make a riddle out of
> an answer.'
>
> KARL KRAUS

The difference between story and plot is another issue that
causes huge confusion for new writers. Look at these two
examples:

> 'The dog came out of the forest. The man left the door
> open.'
> 'The dog came out of the forest. The man had left the
> door open.'

In the first example, is there a link between the two events?
Did the man leave the door open because the dog came out
of the forest? Maybe. What about the second example – does
the tense change make a difference? The answer is yes, it
clearly does. The change of tense in the second example suggests a greater connection between the dog coming out of
the forest and the man leaving the door open. Making that
grammatical change from the simple past ('left') to the past
perfect ('had left') tells us that the man's door was left open
before the dog came out of the forest; indeed, the assump-
tion is that the man left the door open precisely because he

knew the dog would come out of the forest and was waiting for it to do so. The connection in the first example is more tenuous. It may be the case that the man saw the dog leave the forest and opened his door as a result, or it could be that the two events are not connected at all – the link between the two events is not strong.

In this example, the first quotation is a story, the second a plot, and this cause and effect in the second example is

In a plot, things happen because of what has come before, not in spite of it

what defines a plot. In a plot, things happen *because of* what has come before, not *in spite of* it; in a story, however, things 'just happen'. Think of the way children tell stories – they have little sense of plot: 'This happened and then this happened and then this happened . . .' Children have yet to learn how to order events for the benefit of the listener; the chronology of events is preserved but their stories show no sense of causality, and so they remain merely episodic.

Another, much more famous example to show the difference between story and plot was posited by E. M. Forster in 1927:

'The King died and then the Queen died.'
'The King died, and then the Queen died of grief.'

In the first sentence, we understand the order of events but not necessarily the link between them. Did the Queen die *because* the King did? Perhaps not. In the second sentence, however, the link is made strongly and clearly – yes, the Queen died *because* the King did. The second sentence now possesses a sense of causality and we now know the difference between what happens merely consecutively and what happens as a direct consequence of what came before. A story is made out of events, but a plot makes events into a story. Plot leads you through a narrative, whereas you merely follow the story.

Plot leads you through a narrative, whereas you merely follow the story

What is 'narrative'?

The term 'narrative' is a slippery one, refusing to be located or specified. A common response to the question 'What is narrative?' is that it is synonymous with 'story'; another answer is that it is the same thing as plot. While neither response is strictly true, neither is it entirely false. To understand how narratives operate, look at these four sentences:

> 'Peter fell ill.'
> 'Peter died.'
> 'Peter had no friends or relatives.'
> 'Only one person came to Peter's funeral.'

Even in this stripped-down version, we can see the story, but there is a central mystery at its heart: if Peter had no friends or relatives, who was at his funeral? A secret admirer?

A jilted lover? A previously unknown relative? The vicar? This is almost certainly the key to the story, but what happens if you change the order of the sentences? What if you put the last sentence first? Now the whole story becomes a flashback, beginning with the funeral and ending with some kind of falling out between Peter and the other person. Now the story is filled with pathos as the rejected friend/lover/relative thinks back over their relationship with Peter. Likewise, if you put the third sentence first, the story changes again. Now the suggestion is that Peter fell ill as a result of not having any friends or relatives. He pined for human connection but was denied. Then, at his funeral, someone appears, but it is too late. Now the story becomes a tragedy as we identify with Peter's fate. 'There but for the grace of God,' we say, 'go I.'

Despite all this story manipulation, however, we actually have no indication as to the period of time over which this story takes place. These four sentences could have taken three weeks to happen, or three years. Let us say, for the sake of argument, that the story occurs over a period of three months. As a version of Peter's story, how long does it take you to read these four sentences? A couple of seconds, perhaps five? So, it takes approximately five seconds to read about three months of a man's life. Implicit in this idea is that there are two time schemes at play: there is the 'time of the telling' – five seconds – and the 'time of the thing told' – three months. It is precisely this interplay between two time schemes that defines a narrative. Putting one time scheme inside the other is what distinguishes narrative from pure description (which creates space in time) and from pure image (which creates one space in another).

The film theorist Christian Metz has written extensively about what constitutes a narrative and explains the difference between narrative, description and image thus:

> [Compare] these three possibilities: A motionless and isolated shot of a stretch of desert is an image; several partial and successive shots of this desert waste make up a description; several successive shots of a caravan moving across the desert constitute a narrative.

In our definition of what constitutes a narrative, the 'time of the telling' would be synonymous with plot and the 'time of the thing told' with story. The Russian Formalists called story *fabula* and the plot *sjuzhet*; French *narratologistes* call story *histoire* and plot *récit*; Anglo-American Post-structuralists, however, somewhat confusingly refer to plot as 'discourse'. But, by whatever name they are called, the differences between the two are the same. Whatever the story may be, its plot is its engine, its impetus. The causality of a plot ensures forward movement, not circular motion; progression, not repetition. Plot is the driving force within a narrative, moving the reader and the story forward towards the end, while simultaneously delaying that end.

Plot is the driving force within a narrative

Temporal vs plastic

If narratives are defined by their temporal aspect, it follows that only the 'temporal' arts possess narratives. Prose, music, film, theatre, poetry, dance – all these art forms require a 'time of the telling' in order for their stories to unfold; the 'plastic' arts – painting, sculpture, pottery, dressmaking and architecture, for example – do not. You are not required to stand in front of a painting for a specific length of time in order to understand or appreciate it. You may look at a painting for one minute or one hour, it is entirely your decision. A painting does not possess a 'time of the telling', and so when art critics talk about the 'narrative' within a painting, the term is a misnomer since paintings are images and are therefore creating spaces within spaces, not one time scheme within another.

The same issue arises with texts that contain huge tracts of description. An example of a descriptive non-fiction text in its purest form would be an instruction manual or a guide book, which have absolutely no need for a 'time of the telling'. In novels, description works in fundamental opposition to narrative flow. In fiction, when you read a description of a person or place, the 'time of the thing told' pauses and another aspect of writing takes over. Writing description is spending time describing space.

The French *nouveau roman* – Alain Robbe-Grillet's *Jealousy*, for example – extended this style of writing to its logical conclusion. The setting for Robbe-Grillet's novel is a banana plantation in some unnamed tropical country. The story is seen through the eyes of a narrator who is never named (though he is often addressed), never speaks and never acts. The first-person pronoun is never used and the narrator's only role in the novel is to observe the other two characters – his wife and their neighbour (with whom the narrator suspects his wife is having an affair) – in and around the couple's plantation house. The text is full of highly descriptive attention to detail: examining posture and gesture, sometimes in extreme close-up; seeing an action repeated from one or several different points of view; describing the relations between objects in a landscape; noting the progress of shadows thrown by the sun; exploring texture (bark, cloth, paint) and sound. All action is broken down, re-examined, contradicted, and the story is kept at arm's length, pinned down, like a butterfly in a cabinet, never allowed to be more than a *tableau vivant*.

Depicting things in this flat way empties them of human significance and the text becomes a multi-purpose trap for anyone wanting to find meaning. The writing becomes purely self-reflexive and Robbe-Grillet's absent narrator is a blind spot. For his investigations into the pure surface of things, Robbe-Grillet found inspiration in the writings of Raymond Roussel, whose work early in the twentieth century greatly influenced a number of French *nouveau roman* writers who wished to challenge received notions of narrative. Of Roussel's work, Robbe-Grillet wrote:

As there is never anything beyond the thing described . . .
the reader's eye is forced to fall on the surface of things
. . . Such total transparency, which leaves neither shadow
nor reflection behind it, in fact turns into a *trompe l'oeil*
painting. The greater the accumulation of minutiae, of
details of forms and dimensions, the more the object
loses its depth. So this is an opacity without mystery, just
as there is nothing behind the surface of a backcloth, no
inside, no secret; no ulterior motive . . .

Empty enigmas, time standing still, signs that refuse
to be significant, gigantic enlargements of minute details,
tales that turn in on themselves, we are in a flat and dis-
continuous universe where everything refers only to itself. A universe of fixity, of repetition, of absolute clarity,
which enchants and discourages the explorer . . .

Commercial vs 'literary' fiction

The idea of 'plot' in fiction has traditionally been used
by publishers (and the industry in general) to differentiate between 'literary' and commercial fiction. Somehow,
genre fiction that is plot-driven has, over the years, become
synonymous with poorer quality and it is still regularly ig-
nored when it comes to the big prizes. But, of course, in its
own way, commercial fiction is just as hard to write as anything else. Plot is the 'thrust' of a narrative and its genetic
code – without it, your novel will seem meandering, shape-
less and without purpose. A book that is weakly plotted
feels like it will never get started – and then you think it is
never going to end.

A narrative that is driven by a plot whose chain of events has not been sufficiently linked can end up feeling lifeless and inert, but it is also possible to end up with a plot that is too 'busy'. A plot that is 'cluttered' in this way is over-determined in the sense that each of its plot points possesses a multiplicity of causes and suggests a plurality of meanings. Undeveloped plots can leave the reader feeling bored, but plots that are too busy can leave the reader feeling bewildered, which is just as damaging. So where to draw the fine line between the two?

> 'When I am thickening my plots, I like to think "What if . . . What if . . ."'
>
> PATRICIA HIGHSMITH

When thinking about plotting, the first thing to do is to get your story straight. The story in any narrative has to have a few fundamental questions addressed and answered in order to ensure basic comprehension. Put simply, these are: 'who', 'what', 'when' and 'where' (referring to characters, action, time period and setting, respectively). For now, leave the 'why' (motivation) out of it. Barthes referred to the who, what, when and where of a narrative as its 'denotation', and the why as its 'connotation'. Deciding why the characters do what they do is the reader's job, but the denotation is a writer's first business – what's going to happen? To whom? When? Where? These

Deciding why the characters do what they do is the reader's job

are the basic components of your story and they need to be sorted out before anything else.

Once you have your story, you need to decide in what order you're going to place those events. Putting them in different orders will create different effects. Even in our very simple example of three months in the life of Peter, placing events in three different orders created three different effects. Are you going to tell your story logically or chronologically? Plot is the logic and dynamic of narrative, and this logical dynamic is not duty-bound to preserve chronology. You can scramble time in your efforts to tell a story, switching events around in order to ensure the smooth flow of the emotional aspect of your story in the mind of the reader.

Are you going to tell your story logically or chronologically?

Crime novels are a good example to look at when talking about 'plot' as they are perhaps the most purely plot-driven kind of fiction. Other kinds of fiction answer their denotative questions almost immediately, but crime fiction places the who, what, when and where under scrutiny from the outset. The point of a crime novel is to delay these answers until the end of the narrative. Some pose a series of questions that look forward into the future for their answers; others work by asking questions that delve into the past. Anticipatory narratives operate via surprise and suspense and are usually labelled 'thrillers'; retrospective narratives work via the set-up and solution to a mystery and are called 'whodunits'. The logic of the whodunit necessitates that a body turn up at the beginning of its narrative (although, thanks to our meticulous plotting, the murder may not have occurred at the beginning of the story), and proceeds by ranging back and forth over time from this initial effect to find its cause. Thrillers, however, usually work by making us identify closely with the hero at the beginning of the story and then keeping us in close proximity with them as they work from cause to effect and eventually arrive at the truth, preserving chronology along the way. In essence, the basic question of philosophy (and psychoanalysis) is the same as that in crime fiction: who is guilty?

As a writer, Hemingway preferred the world of soldiers and hunters rather than crooks and cops, but his short story 'The Killers' is one of the best crime short stories there is. Two men in black overcoats and derby hats enter a diner in a small town. The owner asks them for their order, but the two men do not know what they want and prevaricate. It eventually transpires that they are there to assassinate one of the regulars at the diner. What follows is a masterclass in veiled threats and subtle shifts in power as the two men assert their authority and control over the owner, the cook and a customer called Nick Adams – all done almost entirely through menacing, Pinteresque dialogue. The situation is a kind of foreshortened version of Michael Haneke's film *Funny Games*, with violence threatening to erupt at any time and the story seething with tension. And all this in just six pages.

If something happens once, it is an accident; but if it happens twice, it is a pattern

For highly plot-driven genre fiction like this, the plot is advanced through words and actions rather than by any reflection on the character's part (this is Hemingway's signature style in his early stories). If something happens once, it is an accident; but if it happens twice, it is a pattern. Such repetition of events can mark changes, both in the story and to characters. Plotting is all about the patterning of events in order to create effects. Switching events around can cause little bombs of surprise and suspense to detonate in different places in your narrative. Such moments of surprise and suspense are the points around which the plot turns. Plot shows us the cogs and pulleys of narrative, the *j'accuses* and, eventually, the *mea culpas*.

Plotless narratives

Of course, not all narratives must, or indeed do, conform so strictly to the demands of 'plot'. I think of thrillers, and other examples of genre fiction that are highly plot-driven, as 'concave' narratives, in the sense that if you look at the structure, it is like looking through a lens that greatly concentrates the 'time of the thing told' (story) and the action. It follows that a 'convex' narrative would do the opposite, spreading the narration out, lengthening the time of the telling and slowing down the story's events (regardless of how long the story actually took to happen). Narratives looked at through a convex lens in this way usually pay much less attention to 'plot', preferring instead to dwell on deep interiority. Such character-led narratives are usually labelled 'literary' fiction.

It has been said, for example, that the structure of *Waiting for Godot* is such that Samuel Beckett left himself free to lay down his pen at any moment. The same applies to the viewer and the reader, who are both free to walk away from the text at any moment without losing too much understanding of the play's themes or message (if there are any). This is because the play is without a discernible plot. Yes, characters come and go (although some cannot), and a few things happen, but the audience is largely no wiser by the play's end than they were at the beginning.

Mike Leigh's *Naked* and Mike Figgis' *Leaving Las Vegas* are other examples of texts that do not have a plot. Of course, these films are narratives, in the sense that it takes us a certain amount of time to follow the story, which takes time to happen, but they are not stories that are made up of a linked series of events. Instead, the events in the stories 'just happen', one after the other, depending on what the capricious main character spontaneously decides to do. They are 'episodic' narratives, more accurately labelled 'chamber pieces' or 'character studies'. The roots of such narratives go much further back, of course: the story of the Immobilised Man can be seen in existential literature (Jean-Paul Sartre's *Nausea* and Albert Camus' *The Outsider*, for example), further back to Knut Hamsun's *Hunger*, and even further back than that, ultimately to the work of Fyodor Dostoyevsky.

Aristotle's Ars Poetica

The first attempt at literary analysis of narrative and what constitutes story and plot was the *Ars Poetica* of Aristotle (384–322 BC). This is the ur-text, the first and foremost piece of literary criticism on which all Western thought and writing on narrative that followed is based. In it, Aristotle, too, differentiated between 'plot' (*mythos*) and 'story' (*logos*), defining plot as 'the ordered arrangement of the incidents'. Many other terms and ideas Aristotle wrote about (particularly in Chapters 6 to 18) have entered the language and are still in common use today, including *in medias res*, *deus ex machina*, *hubris* and *hamartia*. In Chapter 6, he separates out the basic elements of tragic drama into plot, character, diction, thought, spectacle and song. 'Of these elements,' he says, 'the most important is the plot, the ordering of incidents; for tragedy is a representation, not of men, but of action and life.' In this chapter, he also formulates what is probably his most famous idea, namely *catharsis*, which he defined as a kind of spiritual cleansing 'presented in the form of action, not narration; by means of pity and fear bringing about the purgation of such emotions'.

In Chapters 7 and 8, he discusses the fact that a plot must have 'a beginning, a middle and an end', and states that the plot should promote the unity of action above character: 'the plot of a play, being the representation of an action, must present it as a unified whole'. Chapter 10 draws a distinction between 'simple' and 'complex' plots, saying that 'a reversal or a discovery . . . should develop out of the very structure of the plot, so that they are the inevitable or probable consequence of what has gone before, for there is a big difference between what happens as a result of something else and what merely happens after it'.

So much emphasis did Aristotle place on the importance of plot that, more than two thousand years later, the crime writer Dorothy L. Sayers would say of Aristotle, after reading his *Poetics*, that 'what, in his heart of hearts, he desired was a good detective story'. She goes on to say, 'The *Poetics* remains the finest guide to the writing of such fiction that could be put . . . in the hands of an aspiring author.'

Aristotle's 'beginning, middle and end' is the blueprint for much of the narrative drama throughout Western history, right up to the present day – including Hollywood. One of the many gurus of screenwriting, Syd Field, drew a diagram based on Aristotle's *Poetics* to illustrate the basic three-act structure of most Hollywood movies:

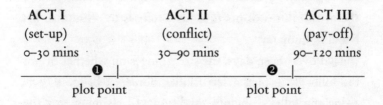

ACT I	ACT II	ACT III
(set-up)	(conflict)	(pay-off)
0–30 mins	30–90 mins	90–120 mins

❶ plot point   ❷ plot point

Field's term 'plot point' is just another name for Aristotle's terms 'discovery' or 'reversal' and is a 'point of no return' in the story – one of many moments that are part of the continual process of elimination that we talked about in the Planning chapter. In a more specific way, it also refers to a key moment just before the end of an act that naturally brings about a partial closure of events in that act but also precipitates and propels the next act into play.

> 'Directing is really about three things: your editing behaviour over time, and then controlling moments that should be really fast and make them slow, and moments that should be really slow and make them fast.'
>
> DAVID FINCHER

As an example of this three-act structure in operation, let us look at David Fincher's gloomy but extremely well-made thriller *Se7en*, in which two homicide detectives work to catch the killer of an obese man who has been force-fed to death. Somerset, played by Morgan Freeman, is world-weary and is due to retire in seven days; in contrast, Mills, played by Brad Pitt, is new to homicide and, despite the dreadfulness of his first case, refuses to relinquish his belief in humanity.

Told over seven days, the story hinges on whether or not the killer is, in fact, a serial killer. Somerset believes he is, citing the killer's obvious erudition and claiming that the killer's victims will turn out to be paradigms of the seven deadly sins. Mills disagrees. If Somerset is right, he guesses the killer will strike again, and soon, so time is of the essence and both cops work round the clock to solve the case and make an arrest.

A scene-by-scene breakdown of *Se7en* illustrates particularly well how the plot points in Field's model exactly match the crucial moments in the plotting of *Se7en,* i.e. whether or not the killer is a serial killer and discovering his identity.

Act I (Set-up)

- Somerset getting up/ready.
- Visits scene of crime – character 'reveal' via colleague. Mills arrives.
- Slight conflict in street.
- Somerset in bed, metronome.
- Titles.

Monday
- Mills gets up/ready.
- Meets up with Somerset.
- First murder scene, Somerset pulls rank on Mills.
- Scene in car where Mills asks Somerset not to jerk him off.
- Forensic report.
- In office with Police Chief. Conflict because Somerset thinks the murders will go on and on.

Tuesday
- Newspaper headlines – death of Defence Attorney.
- DA gives press conference.
- Mills at crime scene of second murder. (GREED)

- Somerset's office. Chief tells him of Defence Attorney's murder. Somerset at odds with city. Chief gives Somerset shards of plastic.
- Somerset goes back to first crime scene, note behind fridge.
- Police station. Somerset shows Chief and Mills Milton quote and photo. (GLUTTONY) Serial killer confirmed. **[Plot Point 1]**
- Knife in dartboard.

Act II (Conflict)

- Somerset in library intercut with Mills at home looking at photos.
- Somerset drops notes on Mills' desk.

Wednesday
- Mills reads Dante in car.
- Enters Somerset's old office, hides Chaucer. Phone call, invitation to dinner.
- Somerset meets Tracey, she is the go-between. Dinner. Ice is broken. Somerset and Mills talk about killings.
- They talk to wife of official. Painting upside down.
- Back to second crime scene.
- Fingerprint office. Corridor.

Thursday
- Asleep in corridor.
- Chief briefs cops on 'Victor'.
- Conversation in car about taking bullets/shooting people.

- Building stormed.
- Victor's room. (SLOTH)
- Waiting outside crime scene, Mills gets emotional. Disguised as a reporter, John Doe takes photos, Mills gives his name.
- Hospital doctor hints at atrocity.
- Tracey rings Somerset that night.

Friday
- Somerset and Tracey in diner, conversation about kids.
- Police station, seven sins on blackboard. Mills out of his depth. Somerset gets idea about library from Mills.
- Library.
- Diner. Informer arrives.
- Barber's. Somerset tells Mills about FBI's 'flagged' books.
- Car. They go through addresses.
- John Doe's apartment. Long chase, Doe lets Mills live. **[Midpoint]**
- Back to apartment, Mills breaks door down.
- Mills pays off witness.
- In room, they find photos. Phone call, photo of blonde.

Saturday
- Leather shop.
- Body in porn shop. (LUST)
- Interview rooms. Mills interviews porn shop owner; Somerset interviews client.

- Bar scene illustrating differences between Mills and Somerset.
- Mills gets into bed, tells Tracey he loves her.
- Somerset in bed, throws metronome across room. Throws knife in dartboard (three times).

Sunday
- Doe calls police – 'I've done it again'.
- Model's room. (PRIDE) Sleeping pills and phone glued to hand.
- Doe arrives in cab.
- Doe walks into police station. **[Plot Point 2]**
- Bloody fingerprints. Chief briefs Mills and Somerset – 'For the first time ever, you and I are in complete agreement'.

Act III (Pay-off)

- Lawyer gives conditions. Unidentified blood on Doe's person.
- Shave off hair.
- Put on bulletproof vests.
- Doe brought to them.
- Car ride. Mills and Doe do all the talking, Somerset watches, listens and waits. Pylons, wide open space. They stop. Van arrives, Somerset meets it, box, Somerset runs. Doe tells Mills about his wife, that he envies his simple life (ENVY), about her pregnancy. Mills shoots Doe. (WRATH)

- Mills taken away. Somerset says he will be 'around', quotes Hemingway in voiceover.

Myths and fairytales

> 'A dead myth is called allegory.'
>
> MICHEL TOURNIER

The Greek version of a familiar myth starts with Artemis, goddess of the hunt and fierce protectress of innocent young women. Artemis demands that Callisto, 'the most beautiful', and her other handmaidens take a vow of chastity. Zeus tricks Callisto into giving up her virginity, and she gives birth to a son, Arcas. Zeus' jealous wife Hera turns Callisto into a bear and banishes her to the mountains. Meanwhile, Arcas grows up to become a hunter and one day happens on a bear that greets him with outstretched arms. Not recognising his mother, he takes aim with his spear, but Zeus comes to the rescue. He transforms Callisto into the constellation Ursa Major, or 'great bear', and places Arcas nearby as Ursa Minor, the 'little bear'.

As the Iroquois of the north-eastern United States tell it, three hunters pursue a bear. The blood of the wounded animal colours the leaves of the autumnal forest. The bear then climbs a mountain and leaps into the sky. The hunters and the animal become the constellation Ursa Major.

Among the Chukchi, a Siberian people, the constellation Orion is a hunter who pursues a reindeer, Cassiopeia.

Among the Finno-Ugric tribes of Siberia, the pursued animal is an elk and takes the form of Ursa Major.

Although the animals and the constellations may differ, the basic structure of the story does not. These sagas all belong to a family of myths known as the Cosmic Hunt that spread far and wide in Africa, Europe, Asia and the Americas among people who lived more than fifteen thousand years ago. Every version of the Cosmic Hunt shares a core story-line – a man or an animal pursues or kills one or more animals, and the creatures are changed into constellations.

According to Frenchman Georges Polti (in a book published in English in 1916), there are a total of thirty-six dramatic situations in all fiction, including such variants as 'Supplication', 'Vengeance of a crime', 'Fatal imprudence' and 'Conflict with a god'. Others say that there are actually only seven original classical or mythological stories and that all others are merely variations of these themes. The seven are the stories of Achilles, Candide, Cinderella, Circe, Faust, Orpheus, Romeo and Juliet, and Tristan and Isolde. Still others say that there are, in fact, only three stories: boy meets girl; boy loses girl; man hunts whale. Finally, there are some who say that all stories can be reduced to two basic types: 'the hero leaves home' and 'a stranger comes to town'. Respectively, these are the 'quest' narrative and the 'siege' narrative.

All stories can be reduced to two basic types: 'the hero leaves home' and 'a stranger comes to town'

While such rigid and drastic classification may be interesting only as an exercise, it is certainly true that 'quest' and 'siege' narratives are actually very prevalent models that have been used throughout the history of literature. Homer's *Iliad*, for instance, is clearly a 'siege' narrative, and his *Odyssey* is a 'quest'. These works are thought to have been written in the ninth century BC, which makes them the oldest extant works in European literature. The fourteenth-century Middle English alliterative romance *Sir Gawain and the Green Knight* is most definitely a quest narrative, as are *Tom Jones*, *Jane Eyre*, *Star Trek* and *Finding Nemo*, to name but a few. Typical siege narratives include *Hamlet*, *Hunger*, *Alien* and *High Noon*.

These prototype stories are repeated endlessly. Take the film *Pretty Woman*, for example. What is the story? A rich businessman hires a prostitute, he falls in love with her and she is transformed into a beautiful woman. Does the 'rags to riches' storyline sound familiar? It should do, as the film is clearly a version of the Cinderella story. The stories of many very old myths and fairytales have been retold in this way throughout time. The story of Achilles, with his famously vulnerable heel, is retold as *Superman*, whose only source of weakness is exposure to Kryptonite; the deluded but chivalrous Don Quixote is reincarnated in the character of Alvin Straight, who sets off on a journey from Iowa to Wisconsin on his lawn mower in David Lynch's *The Straight Story*; Mephistopheles makes a reappearance in *Wall Street* as Gordon Gekko, who espouses that 'greed is good' and tries to persuade Bud Fox to sell his soul for money and power; Orpheus' doomed journey into the underworld to retrieve his lost love, Eurydice, is reproduced in Stanley Kubrick's *Eyes Wide Shut*; and 'star-cross'd lovers' Romeo and Juliet find modern equivalents in Rose and Jack in *Titanic*.

The original stories in myths and fairytales such as these are like bits of glass found on a beach, worn down by time but continually thrown up by the sea. They are the detritus of literature, cropping up repeatedly throughout history precisely because they are sophisticated lessons in morality and conduct. These stories are our masterplots, the mythological structure of society, told to us in various guises from a very early age, there not just to entertain, but to educate, too. In his book *The Uses of Enchantment*, Bruno Bettelheim looks at the Jungian archetypes and Freudian theories underlying many of our best-known fairytales, arguing that the darkness in these stories actually helps children to come to terms with very adult notions such as death, betrayal and murder. These stories prepare young children for adulthood and aid them to integrate themselves into the world.

> *Myths and fairytales . . . are the stories that have the purest plots and . . . the most archetypal characters*

The kinds of stories that show themselves to be most easily classifiable when reducing them to their elements are inevitably myths and fairytales because these are the stories that have the purest plots and that employ the most archetypal characters. But this does not mean that stories cannot cross genres. In his essay entitled 'The Wings of Henry James', James Thurber recounts the evening in a New York bar when Dashiell Hammett revealed that he had taken his inspiration for *The Maltese Falcon* from Henry James' novel *The Wings of a Dove*. Looking at the novels closely, you begin to see the similarities: both feature fabulous fortunes (jewels and an inheritance, respectively); both plots revolve around a swindle; Kate Croy and Brigid O'Shaughnessy both lose their lover. Miles Archer in *The Maltese Falcon* was named after Isabel in James' *The Portrait of a Lady*, and Mr Cairo was so called because James had originally decided to use Cairo, not Venice, as one of the main settings in *The Wings of a Dove*. Or perhaps, as Thurber says, it is all just 'one of those rococo coincidences'.

> *'The story – from* Rumpelstiltskin *to* War and Peace *– is one of the basic tools invented by the mind of man, for the purpose of gaining understanding. There have been great societies that did not use the wheel, but there have been no societies that did not tell stories.'*
>
> URSULA LE GUIN

Propp's 'Morphology of the Folktale'

One of the most fascinating and convincing demonstrations of the underlying, homogeneous nature of all plots is the Russian theorist Vladimir Propp's *Morphology of the Folktale*. In the 1920s, Propp looked at more than a hundred folktales and drew up a chart, or 'morphology', of their basic elements. He first of all noted that there were up to only seven basic character roles. Here they are with the corresponding characters from the first *Star Wars* trilogy:

Hero: Luke Skywalker
Villain: Darth Vader
Donor: Obi Wan Kenobi
Provider: the Force
Dispatcher: Luke's uncle
Helper: Hans Solo/Chewbacca/Yoda
Princess: Leia

He then made a list of what he called the thirty-one basic 'functions'. Not all the folktales included every single function, but the overall shape of all the tales remained the same. The functions are:

1 A member of the family leaves home or is absent.
2 A restriction of some kind is placed on the hero.
3 The hero violates that restriction.
4 The villain tries to find the hero.
5 The villain secures information about the hero.
6 The villain tries to trick the hero into trusting him.
7 The hero falls for it.
8 The villain hurts the hero's family, or one of the family desperately lacks something.
9 This injury or lack comes to light and the hero must act.

10 The hero decides upon a course of action against the villain.

11 The hero leaves home.

12 The hero is tested in some way and, as a result, receives a magical agent or helper.

13 The hero reacts to the actions of the future donor.

14 The hero uses the magical agent or the helper aids him.

15 The hero is led to what he is looking for.

16 The hero fights the villain.

17 The hero is wounded or marked in some way.

18 The villain is defeated.

19 The injury or lack (in no. 8) is put right.

20 The hero returns.

21 The hero is pursued.

22 The hero is saved from this pursuit. (Propp notes that many of the folktales ended here.)

23 The hero returns home, unrecognised.

24 A false hero makes false claims.

25 A difficult task is set for the hero.

26 The task is accomplished.

27 The hero is recognised.

28 The false hero or villain is exposed.

29 The hero is transformed in some way.

30 The villain is punished.

31 The hero is married and/or crowned.

What is remarkable about Propp's morphology is how well it can be applied to all kinds of story from any period. Let's take *Sir Gawain and the Green Knight* as an example, looking at a synopsis of its plot in Proppian terms.

On New Year's Day in Camelot, King Arthur's court is feasting and exchanging gifts. A large Green Knight armed with an axe enters the hall and proposes a game. He asks for someone in the court to strike him once with his axe, on condition that the Green Knight will return the blow one year and one day later (4). Sir Gawain, the youngest of Arthur's knights and nephew to the king, accepts the challenge (5) (6) (7). He severs the giant's head in one stroke, expecting him to die. The Green Knight, however, picks up his own head, reminds Gawain to meet him at the Green Chapel in a year and a day (New Year's Day the next year) and rides away (8) (9) (10).

As the date approaches, Sir Gawain sets off to find the Green Chapel and complete his bargain with the Green Knight (11). His long journey leads him to a beautiful castle where he meets Bertilak de Hautdesert, the lord of the castle, and his beautiful wife (12); both are pleased to have such a renowned guest. Gawain tells them of his New Year's appointment at the Green Chapel and says that he must continue his search as he only has a few days remaining. Bertilak laughs and explains that the Green Chapel is less than two miles away and proposes that Gawain stay at the castle (13).

Before going hunting the next day, Bertilak proposes a bargain to Gawain: he will give Gawain whatever he catches, on condition that Gawain give him whatever he might gain during the day. Gawain accepts. After Bertilak leaves, the lady of the castle, Lady Bertilak, visits Gawain's bedroom to seduce him. Despite her best efforts, however, he yields nothing but a single kiss. When Bertilak returns and gives Gawain the deer he has killed, his guest responds by returning the lady's kiss to Bertilak, without divulging its source. The next day, the lady comes again, Gawain dodges her advances, and there is a similar exchange of a hunted boar for two kisses. She comes once more on the third morning, and Gawain accepts from her a green silk girdle, which the lady promises will keep him from all physical harm. They exchange three kisses. That evening, Bertilak returns with a fox, which he exchanges with Gawain for the three kisses. Gawain keeps the girdle, however (14).

The next day, Gawain leaves for the Green Chapel with the girdle. He finds the Green Knight at the chapel sharpening an axe (15), and, as arranged, bends over to receive his blow (16). The Green Knight swings to behead Gawain, but holds back twice, only striking softly on the third swing, causing a small nick on his neck (17). The Green Knight then reveals himself to be the lord of the castle, Bertilak de Hautdesert (18), and explains that the entire game was arranged by Morgan le Fay, Arthur's enemy. Gawain is at first ashamed and upset, but the two men part on cordial terms (19) and Gawain returns to Camelot (20), wearing the girdle in shame as a token of his failure to keep his promise with Bertilak (21). Arthur decrees that all his knights should henceforth wear a green sash in recognition of Gawain's adventure (22).

Of course, I am not suggesting that anyone should slavishly follow Propp's morphology, but it is a brilliant, illuminating way to see how a plot works in practice. Reading Propp's morphology in tandem with *Sir Gawain and the Green Knight* shows how well its author had laid the traps and sprung the surprises. The beauty of the tale is that while the story initially seems to be about one thing – the beheading game – it turns out actually to be about something else entirely – temptation.

Stories these days might not be original, but they can still be authentic

Ultimately, every story has its own personality. Plot may be the genetic code of a text, but, just as human beings who share 99.9 per cent of the same DNA are obviously and wildly different from each other, so books that show their common lineage are also peculiarly and stubbornly individual. Thank goodness for that. There are very many stories that follow more or less the same plot, but it is the writer's task to create stories, not copy plots. Stories these days might not be original, but they can still be authentic.

Chatman's diagram

Now that we have looked at stories that are (or are not) driven by 'plot', and have defined what a narrative is, let us look inside a narrative to see what is going on. The best-known and most useful attempt to identify accurately the complex set of interactions between a writer and a reader through a work of fiction is the following diagram suggested by Seymour Chatman:

NARRATIVE TEXT

Real	Implied		Implied	Real
→	→ (Narrator) →	(Narratee) →		→
author	author			reader	reader

Chatman proposed this diagram primarily because he wanted to illustrate the differences between 'author' and 'narrator', terms that are often mistakenly thought to be one and the same. It is convention to ignore the real author (D. H. Lawrence's 'Trust the tale, not the teller'), but it is impossible to disregard the narrator. It does not matter if the narrator of a story is a character who plays a significant role within it (Marlow in Conrad's *Heart of Darkness*, for example), or whether the narrator is a character who takes no real part in the action (Nick Carraway in Fitzgerald's *The Great Gatsby*, for instance), or whether the narrator is not actually a character in the story at all (as in Hemingway's early stories), the fact of the narrator's presence is indisputable.

The 'implied author'

'I have a twin brother. And when I was two years old, one of us – the other one – was kidnapped. He was taken to

a faraway place and we haven't seen each other since. I
think my protagonist is him. A part of myself, but not me.'

HARUKI MURAKAMI

The term that is hardest to get a grip on in Chatman's diagram is the 'implied author', coined by literary theorist Wayne Booth. As we have seen, there is a difference between author and narrator, but what defines that difference? Only a handful of writers are in the public eye, and readers will obviously have some idea of what kind of people those writers are. When a writer acquires a high media profile, celebrity can outweigh craft and it is often hard for their readers to continue to believe in that writer's creations. When reading their books, we are too aware of the personality behind them, so much so that the presence of the real author can distract and deter us from the reading process. When fame hits hard like this, writers often complain that their anonymity has been taken from them.

'Wanting to meet an author because you like their work
is like wanting to meet a duck because you like pâté.'

MARGARET ATWOOD

The majority of writers have no such problem, however. Even if a reader knows a few biographical details about a writer before reading their books, they usually do not know very much about them and never will. But this does not stop readers from forming an impression of the author while reading. They might ask themselves, 'What kind of person would write this book?' or 'Why?' The gap between real author and narrator is inhabited by this 'implied author', which is the reader's inkling of what the author must be like based on these impressions and ideas.

Although the author ultimately has no control over what such impressions are, they can still play with this notion. An 'implied author' is a version of the author, their hologram, mask or persona, the person responsible for the design and values of a text. This alter ego could be a twin, a doppelgänger, a dummy, a forger, a decoy or a stand-in, depending on how an author wishes to cast themselves in the minds of their readers. Such play can only really take place if the writer preserves some degree of anonymity, though – it gets proportionally harder the more fixed they become in the public eye.

An 'implied author' is a version of the author, their hologram, mask or persona

But none of this really matters – or at least it shouldn't. As Roland Barthes said, 'a text's unity lies not in its origin but in its destination', i.e. a text is significant only because of where it takes the reader, not where it came from. The author is dead! Long live the author!

The 'narratee'

Just as there is always someone who narrates, so there must equally be a person to whom the narrator addresses the story – the 'narratee'. Usually, the narratee is not identified by name, they are just assumed to be there, present in the narrative so that the story can be heard or read. The very fact that someone listens to, or reads, a story means that it exists – a story simply would not survive without its readers and listeners.

A *story simply would not survive without its readers and listeners*

The most obvious role of the narratee in the text is that of a 'relay' between narrator and reader. Whenever there is an ambiguity within the story, or its narration, the narrator can directly address the narratee with a clarification, knowing that the reader will pick up this information too. Such explicit 'asides' were used a great deal when the novel was in its infancy – by Henry Fielding in *Tom Jones*, for example, and by Laurence Sterne in *Tristram Shandy*. The narratee's role in *Tristram Shandy*, however, is taken a stage further by having the narratee identified as a particular individual, a woman by the name of 'Madam'. While she has no voice of her own in the narrative, we can infer her contributions to the one-sided conversation from the narrator's lines: 'How could you, Madam, be so inattentive in reading the last chapter? I told you in it, *That my mother was not a papist.*'

Since Fielding and Sterne, novelists have given the narratee many other roles to play. In the nineteenth century, for example, 'framed' narratives – whereby one narrative sits inside another – were all the rage. Examples of framed narratives include *Frankenstein*, *Wuthering Heights*, *The Moonstone*, *The Turn of the Screw* and *Heart of Darkness*.

In Conrad's book, the first, unnamed narrator recounts how he once found himself with a group of people waiting on a boat for the tide to turn on the Thames. To pass the time, one of the group, a man named Marlow, proposes to tell them a story, the details of which the anonymous narrator relays to us. Thus Marlow is not the original narrator, and the story he tells is told second-hand. In his own narrative, Marlow is a 'dramatised' narrator, by which I mean he has experienced the events as a character, not merely as an observer. The moment he starts listening to Marlow's story, however, the original narrator becomes narratee and plays no other role for the rest of the story.

Sometimes, the narratee of a story can also be its narrator. In Jean-Paul Sartre's *Nausea*, for example, Roquentin does not intend his narrative to be heard by anyone other than himself because the narrative is comprised solely of his diary, of which he is the only reader. On other occasions, texts may appear to have no narratee at all. The detached prose style in Albert Camus' *The Outsider*, for example, ensures that Meursault remains distant from events in the book, and from himself. The deep solitude that lies at the heart of his character means that Meursault does not know how to interact socially or engage in a real dialogue with anyone, including a narratee. As we read, we have the feeling that his consciousness is turned exclusively outwards, that it has no interior, no 'inside'. The narratee in Camus' book is not sensed either by us or by Meursault himself.

Postmodernism brings back into play a tendency for direct address between narrator and narratee. In Italo Calvino's *If on a Winter's Night a Traveller*, for instance, the narrator addresses the narratee (and, by proxy, the reader) directly throughout the book, beginning: 'You are about to begin reading Italo Calvino's new novel, *If on a Winter's Night a Traveller*. Relax. Concentrate. Dispel every other thought. Let the world around you fade.' For Calvino, this toying with the role a narratee plays in a text highlights the explicitly artificial nature of narrative.

By and large, however, such 'self-reflexive', 'blank' or 'dramatised' roles assigned to the narratee are unusual. In most contemporary novels, it is much more common for writers to assume their stories are naturally being addressed to someone within the textual world, as well as the reader. Unless you deliberately want to start experimenting with form, it is probably safest at this stage to stick with convention.

Conflict

If plot is the engine of a narrative, its heart, then the idea of 'conflict' is its heartbeat

Put simply: without 'conflict' there is no drama, and without drama there is no story. If the fact that a character will find success is never in doubt, there is no interest or involvement for the reader. The gap between desire and its fulfilment is what drives the story and keeps us reading.

Without 'conflict' there is no drama, and without drama there is no story

For writers commencing a novel for the first time, conflict is often overlooked. Very often in the case of new writers, when there is a change in a character's circumstances, this change is brought about extremely easily and without much opposition or many obstacles. Hey presto! Just like that, the character has everything that they have always dreamed of and none of this has come about through their own hard work or at any cost to themselves. It is all too easy.

The effect of this is that the story feels thin and undeveloped, and there can be a predictability to the story that turns it into an undemanding read. The main character might be exposed to drama and tragedy, but the experience does not seem to run too deeply within them. They remain unmarked by events and unmoved by encounters. This makes the reader feel that your main character has no 'inner life', no depth. This is especially true when the character's main goal, the whole purpose for their being, has been built up over a significant amount of time, only to be dispatched in the blink of an eye. We are left feeling underwhelmed, to say the least.

Furthermore, if this lack of conflict within a character also occurs between all the characters in a novel, things can get very dull indeed. If the text is comprised solely of people being nice to each other, exchanging pleasantries, making arrangements, the reader will become bored stiff and will switch off. Happiness does indeed write white.

In order to avoid all of this, you need to put obstacles in the character's path to make life difficult for them. So, for instance, if you want a character to become rich, the first thing you should do is rob them. Their progress cannot be too smooth, so put things in their way in order to prevent them from getting what they want. A locked door, a choice between two lovers, a mistake rued. Each obstacle presents a character with a psychological threshold and, when they reach and pass through that threshold, they are transformed into a different person.

If you want a character to become rich, the first thing you should do is rob them

The trick is to make these obstacles seem insurmountable, but to have the character overcome them anyway. The greater the conflict, the more impressive the effort and eventual outcome. The conflict does not have to be on a grand scale – war, for instance – and every decision does not have to be life-or-death. Conflict can be internal and much quieter, existing on a quotidian level, small scale, as it does in Anita Brookner's *Hotel du Lac*, in which the mind of the main character, Edith Hope, is fully explored as she evaluates herself, how she believes her friends see her, how Mr Neville sees her, and how she eventually sees herself in the light of her experiences at the hotel. Despite Edith's unassuming and self-effacing persona, she privately believes that she has inherited her father's strength of character; by the end of the book, however, she is not too sure.

Conflict within a novel can work on many levels. First of all, there is 'personal' conflict, the fight a person has with themselves. This may be the struggle for spiritual enlightenment, as in the case of Herman Hesse's *Siddhartha*, or it might be the result of a dissatisfaction (as it is for Emma Bovary), or a 'disaffection' – Knut Hamsun's *Hunger*, for example. The point is that the main character feels some kind of 'lack', something wanting inside them that drives them to change their state of being. The stories that work on this kind of conflict can be insightful existential 'portraits' of individuals and often produce great character studies.

Secondly, there is 'interpersonal' conflict, the conflict between two people who, for whatever reason, do not see eye to eye. It could be within a marriage, between a pair of aluminium salesmen in 1950s Baltimore (*Tin Men*), or among soldiers, as in *Platoon*, in which the two sergeants fight over the soul of a greenhorn GI. This kind of conflict is at its most heightened when it is based on a protagonist and an antagonist who have mutually exclusive goals, so that, if the protagonist achieves what they set out to do, it is at the expense of the antagonist, and *vice versa*. One very common example of this kind of conflict is the story of the 'hunter and the hunted', which is the template for countless *Boys' Own* adventure stories: Alexandre Dumas' *The Count of Monte Cristo*, for instance, or Hugo's *Les Misérables*, in which Javert mercilessly and relentlessly pursues Valjean.

A more recent novel that is a good example of conflict is Cormac McCarthy's *The Crossing*. During the novel, Billy Parham crosses the US–Mexico border three times: the first time to release a wolf back into the wild; the second to recover his father's horses; the third to search for his brother. Each time he crosses the border, he loses something – the wolf, the horses, his brother – and he returns home empty-handed. In turn, each loss necessitates that he cross the border again. It is a magnificent novel and one of the best embodiments of pure conflict that I know.

Finally, there is 'social' conflict, which arises between one person and a whole community. In general, this type of story is the result of differently held views, whether it be an individual's non-conformist approach to life (*Crime and Punishment*, for example), or the result of a person maintaining their integrity in the face of great hostility, as in the film *12 Angry Men*. The permutations are endless, but all stories with this level of conflict have in common the idea of 'one person against the world'.

There is another level of conflict, namely that between man and his environment, but as the subject of these stories is usually some form of natural phenomenon, they typically do not pay much attention to character. This kind of conflict is to be found in movies such as *Twister*, *Volcano* and *Armageddon*.

One of the reasons the books that make up the Western 'canon' have endured is because they usually work on more than one of these levels; indeed, some of them work on all three. The initial conflict in *Madame Bovary*, for example, is that Emma Bovary is unhappy with her lot. She believes she deserves a better hand than life has dealt her and she begins to take this frustration out on her husband. Although her husband is loyal, tension grows between them. After two desultory affairs, she has debts that she cannot repay. Her name is tarnished and rumours begin to spread about her affairs. She sinks further into debt and is shunned by the villagers. Her original dissatisfaction has spread out and infected the lives of those close to her and contaminated the community she lives in. Rather than face up to her problems, she drinks arsenic and dies a horrific death.

> '*Writing this book I am like a man playing the piano with lead balls attached to his knuckles.*'
> GUSTAVE FLAUBERT ON *Madame Bovary*

Try this for yourself. Here are the beginnings and endings of three stories. Put in six key events to make it difficult for the characters to get from the beginning to the end. So, beginning scene, then events 1 to 6, then the end scene:

1 A man kills a landlady on a whim and ends up falling in love with a prostitute while serving time.
2 A poor man falls in love with a woman but, many years later, ends up being shot while in a swimming pool.
3 A young girl is taken in by a 'noble' family but ends up being surrounded by police on a heath.

These three examples are actually the beginnings and endings of famous novels – did you recognise them? The first is *Crime and Punishment*; the second *The Great Gatsby*; and the third is *Tess of the d'Urbervilles*.

When placing obstacles for the characters to overcome, an important point to bear in mind is to ensure that those events do not just happen *to* your characters, but that they happen *because of* them. It is easy, and tempting, just to hurl random impediments at characters, but they should in some way be the result of a character's actions and decisions. If something 'just happens' to a character, and they are not seen to act on or react to it, your character will be cast merely as a passive victim of circumstance rather than being an active generator of incident. In this instance, you need to ensure that character determines plot, not the other way round. A character must *achieve* their success, not just acquire it.

'For everything you love you have to pay some price.'
AGATHA CHRISTIE

Plotting your novel is the stage when you should be making sure that your character will not achieve their aims too easily. A good question always to ask yourself when considering this issue is, 'What is it costing the character?' What do they have to give up, exchange or lose in order to get what they want? And does it cost them, not only to get what they want, but to keep it, too? Characters must pay some kind of price for what they desire, and that cost is our investment in their story. If the price is too high and the character fails, the reader may well feel cheated. If the price is high but the character succeeds against the odds, the reader will sense the implausibility. If, on the other hand, the cost is too low, the reader will think, 'Why bother?' It is vital to make sure it is difficult for the characters to achieve their goals – not impossible, just difficult.

> *Characters must pay some kind of price for what they desire, and that cost is our investment in their story*

Resolving conflict brings about change within a character and brings emotional satisfaction to the reader. The conflict resolution in a great many of the best-known stories ends in death, but death does not always resolve issues and is not always the natural endpoint of a story. In *The*

Sheltering Sky, for example, Port's death in the desert provokes an existential 'panic attack' in his wife, Kit. She is crushed by his death, but she is also liberated in a way. The novel continues for another sixty pages as we see the consequences of Kit's loss play itself out in the narrative and, by the end, we realise that the story had been about Kit all along, not Port. His death has not resolved her life, just set her off on a new and different journey. Indeed, endings of stories are, in a sense, just beginnings to other stories. In the most perfectly plotted stories, resolutions give rise to a new set of problems.

> *'I don't believe life is about problems and solutions. I believe it is about dilemmas, and dilemmas don't have solutions; they have resolutions, which then morph and lead you into future dilemmas.'*
>
> PAUL SCHRADER

If you have plotted your story well, and have placed enough obstacles in the character's way so that we enjoy their eventual success as much as they do, your previously 'flatlining' story will now seem full, rich and well developed. The ups and downs in the character's physical and emotional journey will resemble the peaks and troughs of an ECG printout, and you will have breathed life into your story.

So, have confidence in your characters. Give them adversity to overcome – a love lost, a chance missed, a stranger who comes to town. Let their actions and decisions generate the story and not *vice versa*. Show their inner struggle, their struggle in a relationship or within a community, and let the reader revel in the hard-earned and long-delayed outcome of your story.

Have confidence in your characters

Foreshadowing

At the beginning of Jon Amiel's 1995 movie *Copycat*, Sigourney Weaver is giving a lecture about her experiences as a criminal profiler and psychologist working with the police to hunt down and catch serial killers. As she speaks, the camera pans around the audience, picking out faces. Unbeknownst to us, one of the faces is, in fact, the murderer. It is only later on in the film, when the killer's identity is made clear to us, that we think, 'Where have I seen that face before?'

In Peter Høeg's thriller *Miss Smilla's Feeling for Snow*, Smilla finds a cigar box cunningly hidden in a brick wall by a young boy who has fallen to his death from a roof. There are five things in the box: a knife, a harpoon point, a bear claw, a cassette tape and a plastic bus-pass holder. Smilla knows that these objects were precious to the dead boy, and so are significant in some way in helping to discover how exactly he died, but she cannot see how any of the objects can help her. Later, she plays the tape: it is of a man talking to himself in a language Smilla does not understand. There is the sound of cutlery and the hum of a machine in the background, then the tape cuts to white noise.

Smilla thinks nothing more of the tape – it seems meaningless. Much later on in the story, she decides to get an expert opinion on its contents. From one hearing, the expert surmises that the man on the tape is in his mid-forties, from Ammassalik, in East Greenland, and uneducated. He goes on to say that the man is describing a journey across ice, and is talking to a European, because he uses English names for locations. The humming in the background is the sound of propellers. The expert can just make out another voice in the deep background. It is a Dane shouting in English. 'Where in the world,' the expert asks, 'can an East Greenlandic hunter sit and talk in a restaurant, where a Dane is yelling in American English, and where you can hear an airport in the background? Only one place. At Thule Air Base.' The expert analysis proves to be correct and provides Smilla with the lead she needs. She flies to Thule Air Base and, from there, solves the mystery of the young boy's death.

The face in the audience, the tape in the box – these are both excellent examples of 'foreshadowing', the narrative device whereby seemingly innocuous objects later on turn out to be of huge significance. It need not only be an object – it could be a harmless comment, an apparently trivial event, or a person met in passing (as is the case with John Doe in *Se7en*, for instance, who we unknowingly come across when he appears disguised as a photographer). The 'trick' of good foreshadowing is to get the balance right between 'hiding' this significance at the time sufficiently well so that the reader does not guess straightaway, and 'revealing' the existence and presence of the object so that, when its importance is finally revealed, we do not feel that it has arrived out of the blue.

Foreshadowing can be a very effective way of creating surprise and suspense in a narrative, so let us look at the terms 'surprise' and 'suspense' in more detail.

Surprise

A surprise in a narrative is the result of an expectation that is shown to be incorrect. We think something is going to happen, but something else does instead – the plotting has 'wrong-footed' us. We think that this new development was unforeseen, but, on reflection, we realise that had we looked at events from a slightly different angle, it may well have been predicted. Narratively speaking, the operations at work here are subtle and sophisticated, which is why thrillers (in which the element of surprise is the defining feature) continue to be so hugely popular.

> *A surprise in a narrative is the result of an expectation that is shown to be incorrect*

A surprise is the idea of conflict made concrete. Midway through Curtis Hanson's thriller *LA Confidential*, for example, Detective Jack Vincennes visits his captain, Dudley Smith, at his home late one night with a new lead on a shooting at an all-night diner. Vincennes is filling the captain in on this new information when the captain pulls a gun and shoots him dead. This is a huge surprise, not least because playing Vincennes is Kevin Spacey, an actor so well known that we are not expecting him to be killed off so early in the film, if at all.

It transpires, of course, that Vincennes' new information was leading directly to the captain. Hints and clues have been slowly leaked up to this point, but the surprise is so well concealed that nothing could have led us to suspect such a senior figure within the police department. When faced with Vincennes' new lead, the captain has no choice but to act, and this moment of conflict provides the narrative with its biggest surprise. The captain is now revealed as the villain of the piece. In light of this unexpected twist, we assess new clues as the story unfolds, as well as reappraising previous information, until we see that the shooting at the all-night diner does indeed lead to the captain. The pace quickens and the plot thickens. This is good storytelling. In order to work well, a surprise needs to be both unexpected and plausible. Despite its unexpectedness, we realise that it all fits together. If only we had known where to look, we would, in fact, have seen it coming.

Suspense

Suspense is a delay in fulfilling an established expectation. Whereas surprise acts like a small bomb going off in a narrative, suspense is a state of mind, a constant jangling of the nerves, a siren sounding in the narrative. Whereas surprise is all about misdirection, suspense is about delay, and it can come in various forms.

Suspense is a delay in fulfilling an established expectation

There is the straightforward 'question and answer' type of suspense, for instance, found in mysteries and whodunits. Mysteries operate backwards, in that the reader and detective are given all the 'effect' of the crime (the body in the library) at the beginning of the narrative and, while moving forwards, must look backwards in time to find out the 'cause' (the murderer). The overwhelming sense for the reader here is a profound feeling of curiosity.

Another kind of suspense operates in 'dramatic irony', however. As already mentioned, this is the kind of suspense around which most of Hitchcock's films operate. Here, the conclusion to a story is usually foregone, or at least highly predictable. The hero moves closer and closer towards an ending that is going to be surprising for them but not for us. Because we know more about what will happen to the hero than he does, we are not curious about his situation, but we are very anxious about it. We know that the man hiding behind the door with a gun is the 'baddie' – what makes us sweat is that the hero does not know the man is there.

The heroes in Hitchcock's films are usually seeking a particular object, the thing that will save the world from impending doom, but Hitchcock attaches so little importance to the object being sought that he labels it the 'MacGuffin'. Whether it be radioactive chemicals (as in *Notorious*), a code (as in *The 39 Steps*), or microfilm hidden in a figurine (as in *North by Northwest*), its function in the plot remains the same. Hitchcock is more interested in anxious journeys than in endings that satisfy our curiosity.

Another kind of suspense exists in texts in which the character knows more than the reader, usually in the form of a secret buried deep in their past that is eventually revealed. This trait is common to both mysteries and thrillers, but whereas mysteries work by posing a question at the beginning of the narrative – 'Who killed Colonel Mustard?' – thrillers do not start with such a huge narrative question mark. In thrillers, the hero instead stumbles upon the enigma and proceeds from there, living on their wits as they deal with the obstacles thrown at them from all quarters.

The first half of *LA Confidential*, for instance, operates very much as a thriller. In the line of duty, Ed Exley and Bud White stumble across some evidence that points to their captain's involvement in an all-night diner shooting. They proceed with caution, trying to find harder evidence. Vincennes' death is confirmation, and the captain's incriminating secret from deep in his past is finally brought to the surface. From now on, the kind of suspense changes: unbeknownst to Exley and White, the captain had known the reasons for the diner shooting better than anyone, but once that knowledge is unearthed, the narrative switches and becomes a straight 'race against time'.

Foreshadowing is a highly useful tool for a writer, especially in genre fiction, but it is another device that takes time to get right. To give hints of things to come entices the reader and sets up an expectation for them, but there is a fine line between enticement and blatancy. Whenever there is a possibility of a surprise or some suspense being generated in a narrative, new writers tend to scupper their chances by allowing the narrator, or characters, to announce the significance of something 'before the fact'. At moments when clues should be subtly hinted at, they are often turned into 'signposts', with a large arrow pointing to what is going to happen. This, of course, deflates the narrative and robs the reader of any possibility of suspense or surprise.

A story I once read centred on a character who suffered from Poland syndrome. Very early on, the narrator revealed this fact to the reader, but the character had yet to learn of it. When he did find out a hundred pages later, he was, of course, completely surprised, but all the reader felt was irritation at having to wait so long for the character to find this out. This is an obvious example, but it is surprisingly common for new writers to signpost rather than subtly foreshadow that something is about to happen.

Coincidence/credibility/convenience

In another story I once read, two young Germans fall in love, but are then separated by war. Twenty years later, the man finds himself in New York. He is not there on business, he knows no one in the city – there is no real reason for him to be there at all, in fact. As he is walking down a main street in Manhattan, he thinks about his lost love. He knows she went to live permanently in the US, but does not know where. Then, lo and behold, he bumps into her in the street. Amazing! What are the chances? It is a miracle!

Coincidence is one of the most inviting and obvious traps for a first-time writer to fall into. It all seems so logical and natural that two people should 'just happen' to bump into each other in a city the size of New York, but to the reader, nothing could be further from the truth.

Of course, coincidences happen in reality. But fiction is not reality

Of course, coincidences happen in reality. But fiction is not reality. It is difficult for new writers to spot the difference between a character being somewhere for the sake of the plot and a character being somewhere because they have good reason. It was necessary for the young German man to go to the US so that he could meet his lost love again, so the writer has him go there for no other reason. Returning to F. Scott Fitzgerald's idea that character and plot are dual aspects of the same function, it follows that a character's arrival at a place must be the consequence of something that happened beforehand and must be the cause of what happens afterwards.

Set down like this, it is clear that there is an inversely proportional link between a character's reason to go somewhere and a reliance on coincidence to get them there. A surfeit of coincidences in a story is usually the result of a complete lack of character motivation. If, as a writer, you are not sure why characters are doing things, it is tempting to make them 'just happen' to be in the right place at the right time. This is the easiest, laziest route for you to take as a writer. It means that you are not doing your job properly because you are taking a short cut and avoiding the hard work of properly embedding the reasons for your characters' actions.

You may hope that no one will notice, but of course they do. Readers can spot coincidence being used to advance a plot a mile off. Just one whiff of such expediency and you will be guilty as charged. Relying on coincidence to further your story will demolish what Coleridge termed the 'suspension of disbelief' and destroy any confidence the reader has in your abilities as a storyteller.

It is far more dramatic, and believable, if you give a reason for a character to be in a particular place at a particular time. It would have been far more credible, for example, if the writer had made the German man go to great lengths to find out where his lost love was. Perhaps he hires a private investigator, or does the work himself, searching through phone books, city records and employment details, following every clue until, finally, he gets a lead as to her whereabouts. Then, he books a flight and we watch with apprehension as he makes his way over to America to visit her. How will she react? What will she say? Now, the meeting in America is set up, not merely a coincidence. We follow every step of the way as our hero expends a huge amount of energy in search of his lost love. Not only is this whole scene now highly motivated, it is also supremely suspenseful.

Of course, as a writer, you can still employ coincidence as a narrative device – a character can still appear to be somewhere coincidentally when, in fact, they are feigning surprise when they 'just happen' to bump into someone, but this shows *intention* and so it is fine. Whatever the reason, characters should have *motives* for their actions; they must be seen to be actively determining the course of their own life and not just 'floating' through the story, letting things happen passively to them. Remember, 'acting is doing', and the story's direction grows out of what the characters do.

If you feel that you might have one too many coincidences in your story, look back over your manuscript for phrases such as 'suddenly', 'at the same time', 'accidentally' or 'luckily'. The most culpable of these is 'suddenly', a word that has been the cause of thousands of chance meetings. Go back over your plotting and, at every moment, ask yourself not only *what* happens next, but *why*.

'Aristotle makes the distinction between what is possible and what is plausible. A movie does not have to be possible; it has to be plausible. It's not quite possible that the whole story of Oedipus would ever happen; it's only remotely possible. But it is plausible – that is, it satisfies some psychological need in response to a personal notion of what is true. So, therefore, Oedipus is plausible because it should be true, or needs to be true, not because it could be true. And in the same way any fiction should be plausible, though it need not be possible.'

PAUL SCHRADER

As for 'convenience', so there is the same problem with 'credibility'. The contract between reader and author rests on the reader's willingness to suspend their disbelief. For the sake of the story, they will accept as believable, provisionally at least, those events or characters that would otherwise seem incredible. So, your job is to make sure that your characters and events remain as credible as possible.

Again, this is often where new writers slip up. The trap lies in not being able to judge how far to stretch the bounds of credibility. For example, I remember a story in which during a fight the narrator comments that one of the characters pulls out a small knife. There had been no prior mention of this knife, and so the reader immediately thinks, 'Where on earth did this knife come from?' Later on in the same story, a character gains illegal entry into a building by forcing the lock and pushing the door open. Again, the reader's first response here is to ask, 'How exactly did he manage to do that?' It is actually quite difficult to break into a building, yet the character does so with ease. Characters that produce weapons from nowhere and enter buildings at will – there is not a level of reality here that the reader can believe in. Moments that overstretch the bounds of credibility in this way will be picked up on and questioned instantly by the reader. If you do not have the answers, then you have a problem.

Relying on coincidence to further your story and overstretching the bounds of credibility are both indications that you are ordering events to suit your needs, not the needs of the story. It is convenient for you to have a character achieve everything they need with the minimum of effort and exactly on cue, as it were. 'On cue' is the key here. If you look back over your plot and find that everything is happening more quickly and easily than you had planned, chances are that events are happening far too conveniently to be credible.

The notions of coincidence, convenience and credibility are interchangeable to a certain degree, and are really just part of the same big headache. Again, the trick is to try to shake yourself free of thinking in terms of the easiest, laziest routes. If events happen completely 'on cue', there will be little surprise or suspense for the reader, so throw something in to stir up your plot. Make sure that, however unlikely an event may seem, it stays this side of plausible by making the event arise as much as possible out of what preceded it, as well as precipitating what follows. Finally, make sure your characters have their reasons for the things they do. If done successfully, this work will justify the reader's faith in you. Once you have their trust, you will be able to lead them anywhere you like, and not only will they follow, they will do so gladly.

The passage of time
How much time do we need to account for?

Together with deciding on what kind of role you want your narrator to play in the telling of the story, your handling of the passage of time is the other main concern you will have as a writer. Because the passage of time in a narrative is the most novel-like feature of a novel, the thing that defines a novel *per se,* it is the other aspect of fiction over which you need to develop most control.

As we have already seen, all narratives are made up of two time schemes, one inside the other: there is 'the time of the telling' and 'the time of the thing told' – narration and story, respectively. This temporal double helix is what defines a narrative – without it, we have either pure description (spending time describing space) or pure image (creating a space within a space). Since there are two time schemes to consider, your decision regarding how to handle the passage of both produces all sorts of permutations.

Luckily, the French narratologist Gérard Genette has looked in detail at these permutations and has written about the main differences between them. It is useful to go through them.

Summary

'Summary' is the most universal way in which we combine the two time schemes and it occurs when the time of the narration is briefer than the time of the story. Most novels simply do not take as long to read as the events in the story took to happen, so the default setting of most novels is that they are summaries of the stories they are telling.

However, there is a more particular use for summary within a narrative, one whereby the narrator decides to offer us a 'round-up' of events *within* a scene in order to speed up the pace of the narrative, a decision which means that the narrator 'glosses over' such scenes instead of 'getting into' them. For example: 'On arriving home Elizabeth went to her room to have a rest, while Teresa unpacked the trunks'; or 'They finished their tea and went to their rooms to get dressed'; or 'After dinner they went to the drawing room. Teresa continued with the letters and her aunt read the newspaper'. This device is especially common in nineteenth-century 'classical' narratives.

In these kinds of texts, not only does the narrator sometimes sum up events for us *within* a scene, the narrator may also choose to account for all the story-time that passes *between* scenes. For example: 'The next few days passed pleasantly'; or 'During the two weeks after her aunt's death'; or 'Over the next days there was a whirlwind of activity'.

Rather than speeding up the pace of the narrative, the narrator's tendency to 'summarise' the story within scenes, or account for all the time that passes between them, actually slows down the pace because, narratively speaking, these moments are 'dead time', longueurs when the narrative is merely treading water. Anti-dramatic by nature, they neither drive the story forward nor do they provide enough interest in themselves to justify their inclusion.

One of the things you will realise when embarking on a long piece of fiction for the first time is that you simply do not need to round up events for us like this, to account for all the time that passes. Instead, cut to the quick of each scene, and cut to the next scene at the first available opportunity, in order to keep the pacing crisp and the story flowing. Your reader will be eternally grateful if you do.

You do not need to account for all the time that passes

Ellipsis

> 'In order to make the novel into a polyhistorical illumination of existence, you need to master the technique of ellipsis . . . The art of ellipsis is absolutely essential. It requires that one always go directly to the heart of things.'
>
> MILAN KUNDERA

An 'ellipsis' is a period of time left out of the narrative, an elision, an omission. As in the quotation above, ellipses in a sentence are usually marked by three dots, or by a line break (not a new paragraph) between sections within a chapter. The important point to bear in mind is that, technically speaking, an ellipsis is a discontinuity in the *narration*, not the story, so when we come to the three dots, or a line break, it does not mean that there is an interval in the story, but it does mean that a period of time has been left out of its telling.

Another point to bear in mind is that ellipses mark a leap in time, but they do not necessarily mark a shift in space. We may 'cut' forward in time, but we may also 'cut' to another place without any time having elapsed at all, so the term 'ellipsis' only refers to a jump in time, not space.

The use of ellipsis as a literary device is not new. As Seymour Chatman notes, 'Ellipsis is as old as *The Iliad*.' Henry Fielding famously used it to omit twelve years of Tom Jones' life because 'nothing worthy of a Place in this History occurred within that Period'. As a result of the stodginess that summary can create in a narrative, it has largely fallen from favour, but the ellipsis ensures narrative flow and, for this reason, it still retains its sense of freshness and urgency.

A woman arranges to have lunch with her boyfriend and puts the phone down. We then cut to her sitting at the restaurant table – no need to see her get dressed, leave her flat, get on a bus. The idea of *selection* is key. They say you can burn the first two reels (about twenty minutes) of most Hollywood films before the story really gets going, and it is true. Get into scenes as

Get into scenes as late as possible and get out of them as early as possible

late as possible and get out of them as *early* as possible. No need to include the preamble, or the postscript, and definitely no need to report all the details in between.

Scene

Story and its narration are of relatively equal duration here, so the reader experiences the story more or less 'as it happens'. The conventional nineteenth-century novel alternated 'scene' with 'summary' to comprise its narrative, a pattern that many novels have followed ever since. Although many contemporary novels pay much more attention to scenes written in 'real time', it is still rare for a narrative to be written entirely minute by minute. Setting a 250-page novel – which would take approximately ten hours to read – exhaustively around ten consecutive hours in a character's life is a high-risk strategy and, for better or worse, most readers would simply not have the patience.

There are examples of such texts, however. The TV series *24* is an obvious example but there are other, older examples, too. In 1948, Hitchcock filmed a scene-for-scene version of Patrick Hamilton's stage play *Rope*, which is a real-time account of an evening spent by a schoolteacher, among others, at the house of two of his former students. Hitchcock built an elaborate set that could accommodate complicated camera movement, and filmed in real time, so that the only cuts in the finished movie occur when the canisters of film ran out. For a modern audience, the highly theatrical end product is perhaps a little creaky, but it is fascinating nonetheless to see every step of James Stewart's gradual realisation that the students are, in fact, murderers.

Agnès Varda also used a (there or thereabouts) 'real-time' narrative for her film *Cléo de 5 à 7*, which shows us two hours in the life of Cléo as she wanders around the streets of Paris, waiting for the result of a medical biopsy for cancer. Clearly, the pleasures of Varda's film do not lie in a strong plot, but she concentrates her efforts on various other narrative devices and textures – internal monologue, chance encounters, a strong sense of location, lighting – in order to compensate.

Stretch

The time of the telling in this classification is longer than the time of the thing told. When the narration in a narrative is 'stretched' like this, the effect is similar to looking through a convex lens – the story-time remains the same but the narration expands. Again, it is rare for the narration in novels to be longer overall than the story, but there is an argument to say that *Ulysses* is such an example. The novel is set over a period of twenty-four hours, but most readers, if not all, are unlikely to be able to finish the book in that time and so the story-time is 'stretched' for its entire duration.

Handling the passage of time in this way is very common for individual scenes, especially those scenes that constitute moments of 'high drama'. At such moments, it is good practice to slow the narration down so that the reader can absorb the full emotional impact of the scene and pick up every nuance of detail. Not so much, however, that the scene becomes overwrought – just enough so that the reader experiences the full emotional 'weight' of a scene. Key dramatic scenes that pull their punches are very frustrating for the reader.

One of the most famous examples of the stretched scene is the seven-minute Odessa steps sequence in Sergei Eisenstein's film *Battleship Potemkin*, which is extended to an excruciating degree so that we do not miss a thing. As the soldiers fire and descend on the protesters, we see a woman pick up her skirts and run, a man with no legs leaping down steps, a man taking an eternity to fall, the camera moving with the protesters down the seemingly endless flights of steps, an old man on the ground being jumped over, people rolling down the concrete steps. A young boy, oblivious of his mother, is shot and falls over, but she turns and sees him, screaming in terror as someone crushes his hand, while, most famously of all, a pram takes an age to tumble down the steps, forever teetering on the brink of falling over. The whole scene takes longer to happen than would have been the case in reality, creating an unbearable sense of tension.

Pause

This occurs when the story-time stops altogether, although the narration continues. In fiction, we might step out of the action while the narrator pauses to describe a person, object or place. As we have already seen, the narrative is temporarily no longer a narrative because one of its time schemes has stopped. A different kind of writing now takes over – description, which is time spent describing space. Virginia Woolf's novel *To the Lighthouse* has a sixteen-page middle section entitled 'Time Passes', which is a static description of the Ramsay family's Scottish holiday house over an extended period of many years. There is no action in the section, no dialogue, just a long series of descriptions of the house and its environs.

In cinema, the 'freeze frame' is an example of a moment when the time of the thing told stops completely. The effect of a freeze frame is very powerful, especially if it comes at a film's end, when it is held as the final, climactic note. In François Truffaut's *Les Quatre cents coups*, the last image of the film is a freeze frame that catches fourteen-year-old Jean-Pierre Léaud as he sees the sea for the very first time. After a series of disasters and a life of hardship, his joy on the sandy beach is self-evident as the camera freezes on his face. The effect makes us ponder, even more than usual, what life has in store for this young, but resilient, boy.

In *Butch Cassidy and the Sundance Kid*, however, the final freeze frame is used to create a very different effect. Here, the frozen moment is the moment Butch and Sundance run out, guns blazing, to meet their deaths. By the time the film's inevitable outcome has been reached, the characters of Butch and Sundance have worked their way into our affections so much that the makers decide not to show us their gory end. The final image, capturing the moment the odds are stacked too heavily against them, turns to sepia and is held in perpetuity, thus ensuring mythical status.

Flashbacks and flashforwards

We all think we know what the term 'flashback' means, but, like 'narrative', try to define it precisely and it gets more fiddly than you thought. At its most simple, a flashback is a depiction of events understood as having occurred prior to the section that precedes it. It is all to do with comparing time. If a reader were to pick up a book and open it at any point during a flashback, they would not be able to distinguish it from sections of the narrative that were not flashbacks. It is only by temporal difference that we understand what a flashback actually is.

As a literary device, the flashback is nothing new – like ellipsis, it is used in *The Iliad*. Genette also did work on flashbacks, and came up with a useful set of terms to differentiate between them. 'Anachrony' is the general term he used for any kind of temporal 'break'. His term for a flashback proper is 'analepse'; a flashforward is a 'prolepse'. 'Interior' analepses refer to any event happening inside the narration but not already shown, whereas 'exterior' analepses refer to events occurring before the narration's beginning. 'Amplitude' is his term to describe how much of the past is told, and the 'portée' of the analepse is how long ago the past event occurred.

As a storytelling tool, flashback is a device that rearranges, and therefore complicates, plot order. Some flashbacks act merely as a 'story being told' and tend not to be very subjective. They add touches to the story, plugging the gaps in our knowledge of what went on in the past. They can, for example, be used retrospectively to fill in ellipses. This is a relatively straightforward usage of the flashback, but other kinds of flashback can be used in a highly interiorised way, producing something far more subjective and embellished. This kind of flashback is typically used as a means of representing memory, dreams or fantasy. Ingmar Bergman's film *Wild Strawberries* is a beautiful example of how memories and dreams are woven into everyday reality to conjure the inner life of seventy-eight-year-old Professor Isak Borg. Flashbacks can thus be used in a much more elaborate way, as a contributor to the *style* of the novel, not just the story.

When there is a juncture in the narrative between present and past, the join can become a complex interface between memory and history. At that moment in time, there is the character as a 'subject in history', but there is also the character's relationship with the retelling of their past. Whatever we have experienced in life sinks into our memory and is foreshortened by it. Later, it might be called to mind again and set against a different background, with the result that the subject is able to develop hitherto unforeseeable connections between past and present. The memory recalled, however, can never assume its original shape, because this would mean that memory and perception were identical, which is clearly not the case. A new setting brings to light certain aspects of what we had committed to memory, and these bits of memory, in turn, shed light on the next new scene or setting we encounter. These connections are the product of the subject's mind working backwards and forwards against each new event. We call this merging of memory and history 'subjective memory'.

Subjective memory is a highly effective means of complicating time and exploring identity

Subjective memory is a highly effective means of complicating time and exploring identity. D. M. Thomas' novel *The White Hotel* is a good case in point, delving into, as it does, what constitutes subjectivity, and how that subjectivity is constructed by historical events and by the individual's reaction to those events.

The narrative is divided into six parts, the first of which is actually a long, highly erotic prose poem that we later discover was written on a score for *Don Giovanni*. The second section is a journal, a prose version of the same events. In the third section, Sigmund Freud introduces his case study of a woman called Frau Anna G., an opera singer who has come to him complaining of pains in her breast and womb. Up until now, we have had no reference points to guide us through the story, nothing by which to judge what is 'story', what is 'narration' or what is memory, dream or fantasy.

It isn't until the fourth section, well over halfway through the novel, that we meet the 'real' main character – Lisa Erdman – for the first time. This meeting reshuffles the time schemes in our head and we realise that 'Anna G.' is Freud's pseudonym for Erdman and that the first two sections were Lisa's fantasies that Freud had asked her to write down. We deduce that this must have happened after the third section, so we have begun the novel with a 'flashback-fantasy'. This third section, the Freudian case study, explores her deep past and the fourth section returns to the present day. In the fifth section, we once again follow Lisa in the present day as she gets caught up in the deportation of Jews from Kiev in September 1941. The final section is a coda: a kind of dream, or maybe a (death)wish fulfilment. We are never sure.

If it shows anything, the dream-like narrative of *The White Hotel* demonstrates that time is once again treated as an element to be shaped and shifted. The present is in the past, the past in the present – temporality is subjective and relative. The novel's exploration of the unconscious ultimately escapes the level of 'psychological realism' inherent in the character of Lisa Erdman and becomes the subject of the narrative itself. The Russian-doll-like structure of the narrative means that we never discover the truth of Lisa Erdman; her character constantly eludes us, just as her own past eluded her.

'Time interests me tremendously because there is such
confusion in it. It is only something we have invented
for ourselves. It's a trap. I wanted to destroy that trap.'
NIC ROEG

Pauline Kael described Nic Roeg's 1973 film *Don't Look Now* as 'The fanciest, most carefully assembled enigma yet put on screen.' The story centres on a couple, John and Laura (played by Donald Sutherland and Julie Christie), whose daughter, wearing a shiny red mac, has recently drowned in the pond at the family home. They go to Venice, where John is restoring a church, to recuperate. There, Laura meets a blind woman who is a 'seer' and who tells her that her husband is in mortal danger because he refuses to acknowledge that he, too, has the gift of second sight. Meanwhile, a tiny figure dressed in a shiny red mac keeps on catching John's eye. Knowing it is not his daughter, but thinking that it is another child in danger of drowning, he is determined to save her.

What follows is a series of fragmented clues – glimpses of red, a funeral procession, breaking glass, a cry in the night – all of which meld into an awful sense of impending doom. What John does not grasp is that he is seeing the chronicle of his own death foretold and this sense of *déjà vu* is an intense coupling of memory and prophecy. Right up to the very last moments of the story, the funeral procession is puzzling for the viewer. Whose is it? We do not understand what we are seeing. Bizarrely, these flashforwards are only understood in retrospect; it is only once we have arrived at the moment in the story from which the flashforward commenced that we understand that it was a flashforward at all, and the film reveals its meaning only at the moment the viewer plunges through the trapdoor into the abyss of madness.

Flashforwards are used far more rarely than flashbacks (they are particularly good at confusing the reader), but they can be an effective method of foreshadowing. In Steven Soderbergh's *Out of Sight*, George Clooney appears in a hotel bar where Jennifer Lopez is being chatted up by some businessmen. He is charming and attentive, succeeding where the businessmen have failed, and we flashforward to see them falling into bed together. Then we cut back to his seduction in the bar and it is only then that we understand we have just seen a flashforward. We now know that, despite herself, Jennifer Lopez is going to fall for his charms. The amplitude and portée of this prolepse are both very small, but the flashforward serves to give us a 'taster' of what is to come, adding a layer of inevitability to a scene that is already full of sexual tension.

Flashbacks in particular are alluring devices for first-time writers. They promise lucidity, profundity, but are mostly used clumsily, taking away from narrative clarity instead of adding to it. Flashbacks provide background information, but they also stop the story dead in its tracks. If a flashback is particularly long, or delves too far back in time, it can do irreparable harm to the narrative flow and reading experience.

The key is to use them very sparingly indeed, and only if you feel it is absolutely necessary. If you think you need a ten-page flashback, chances are you do not. If you find that you can only explain an aspect of your story by including a ten-page flashback, you almost certainly need to rework your plot. In my experience, the most powerful way to use flashbacks is to provide just a brushstroke or two to fill in character detail. Plucking a moment out of a character's past that 'cross-references' the present-day story, or that provides evidence of a consistency of behaviour over time, can be very effective indeed at increasing our sense of who a character is and why they do things.

As a writer, however, allow time for these decisions to develop in your writing, since they are often best made subconsciously. Flashbacks function on a very different level than plot, say, because not only can they be used to clarify aspects of the story, but they also enhance the fabric of a narrative, adding texture and tone, providing light and shade. If used well, they contribute uniquely to a story.

Pace
The current in the river

The pace in a novel is the current in the river – invisible to the eye, but a force on the body. It impacts on readers

The pace in a novel is the current in the river – invisible to the eye, but a force on the body

in subtle, unconscious ways. When people say a book is too long, they usually mean it is too slow.

But 'pace' does not automatically translate as 'speed' – it is more about finding the right pace for your work, however fast or slow. It is the slackness in pace that you want to avoid.

Finding the right pace in the various stages in your novel is intimately connected to plotting on the one hand and editing on the other. If your plotting has been well thought through, the chances are that your pacing will be OK, too. Equally, if you find that you are self-conscious about the pace in your writing, it will almost certainly be 'off'. But however unsure of your pacing you might be while writing your first draft, you can still tweak it when you edit, so just keep going for now.

As you would expect, the pace of a narrative has everything to do with how you handle the passage of time. Chapters can be short or long, but the pace of a chapter involves more than just its length. How much story-time is covered in each chapter? How long do you take to narrate that amount of story? Clearly, if you take ten pages to account for an hour of story-time, the pace of that chapter will be much faster than if you took twenty-five pages. In addition, there is the 'balance' of the overall narrative to consider. Does the story move quickly in the opening chapters, only to tail off in the second half? Does the middle sag?

If you have divided up your narrative into parts, you also have to think about their overarching combination, their 'architectonic clarity', as Milan Kundera terms it. For his novel *Life Is Elsewhere*, Kundera divided his narrative into seven parts and assigned a musical 'tempo' to each, depending on the relationship between how long the part was and how many chapters it included. Part One, for instance, contained eleven chapters in seventy-one pages, so he labelled it *moderato* – or 'at a slow, moderate pace'. With fourteen chapters in thirty-one pages, Part Two was *allegretto* – 'at a fairly quick tempo' – and so on. The complete list of tempi was: *moderato, allegretto, allegro, prestissimo, moderato, adagio, presto*, which translates as medium, quick, quicker, very quick, medium, slow, quick.

Kundera said that the movement from *adagio* in the penultimate part to the *presto* of the final part was the key to the novel. For him, that contrast in pace focused all the emotional power of the novel into the final movement. Symphonies, whose deep structure is often similar to that of a novel, have traditionally been composed by alternating fast and slow movements (rather like the aforementioned alternation of 'scene' and 'summary' in classical narratives), usually ending with a fast, happy movement following a slow, sad one. Kundera makes the similarity explicit.

> *'Speed up for the essential, slow down for the superfluous.'*
>
> UMBERTO ECO

A conventional pacing structure is, of course, not compulsory – anyone can play around with pace and structure to their heart's content and produce stunning effects. Sofia Coppola's film *Lost in Translation*, for example, benefited enormously from her highly individual and unusual approach to the editing. Throughout the film, the viewer senses that something is about to happen – but it never does. The narrative feels as though it has been made up of the bits of film that other filmmakers would have left on the cutting-room floor. Characters stare out of windows or into space, they wake, surf through endless TV channels, swim pointless lengths in the hotel pool, go to sleep. There is an air of listlessness, boredom and numbness to the narrative that reflects the state of being permanently jet-lagged.

In general, writing too much is far more common among new writers than writing too little. This is no bad thing, since all can be trimmed and 'tucked in' later on, but, as a general principle, be wary of 'overwriting' because it plays havoc with the pacing of your piece. Naturally, cutting can speed up the pace. If you feel your pacing is too slow, you can cut scenes that do not push the story forward significantly; you can end chapters or sections earlier; you can trim scenes made up almost entirely of dialogue; you can trim individual lines of dialogue; cut lines of dialogue that are repetitious; avoid making the same point many times over in the dialogue; cut any background information, exposition or historical research that is not absolutely necessary. All this will help.

The temptation for new writers is to spend the longest possible time with each scene, far beyond what you need in order to move the story forward. What you *should* be doing, without compromising the scene's integrity, is spending the *least* amount of time possible with each scene. As I have suggested before, get into scenes as *late* as possible and get out of them as *early* as possible. Move things along quickly, do not hang about. Keep the reader on their toes. Make them have to keep up with events instead of forcing them to twiddle their thumbs while you have your characters overstay their welcome.

Setting
How much does the environment act on a character?

*'Whatever our souls are made of, his and mine are
the same.'*

EMILY BRONTË, *Wuthering Heights*

A setting for a novel should be as 'present' as any of the
characters. In Paul Bowles' *The Sheltering Sky*, for example, the Sahara desert and its 'virulent sunlight' provides
the backdrop for the novel but also takes on an increasingly
claustrophobic, emptying role, smothering love and hope
until all that is left is sand and wind. In this way, the reader should be able almost to 'see' the background of a novel
without even realising it, for without a strong sense of setting,
the fictional world of a novel will seem underdeveloped and
characters will appear unanchored, rootless. Just imagine
if *Ulysses* had not been set in Dublin, if Franz Kafka's *The
Trial* was not set in Prague, or Thomas Hardy's work without Wessex. I particularly love Hardy's *The Return of the
Native* for its wonderful Egdon Heath setting and the red-
dleman Diggory Venn, who lives and works there. All these
places are 'local' to these writers, and their books would be
unthinkable without this strong sense of place.

But, for me, the novel whose story is most indistinguishable from its setting is Emily Brontë's *Wuthering Heights*. When Lockwood visits Wuthering Heights for the first time, he notices 'the power of the north wind, blowing over the edge' by 'the excessive slant' of the 'stunted firs at the end of the house; and by a range of gaunt thorns all stretching their limbs one way, as if craving alms of the sun'. The inhabitants of Wuthering Heights – the Earnshaws – are hard and unrefined. Any culture they acquire is always just an overlay, a surface smoothness that does not alter the hard structure underneath. Heathcliff is an Earnshaw by nature, though not by blood, and his virtues are the Earnshaw virtues: steadfastness, determination and an unswerving dedication to the objects of his devotion. Earnshaws have fierce tempers and an appetite for violence. All these features are felt by the reader in the 'power' of the wind, 'the excessive slant', the 'stunted firs' and the 'gaunt thorns'. Although describing the house, Lockwood could just as well be describing the people who live in it.

Brontë's evocation of place is phenomenal and, in the character of Heathcliff, we get its perfect, total embodiment. In the book, Catherine warns Isabella that Heathcliff is 'an arid wilderness of furze and whinstone'. Heathcliff is less a person and more a force of nature and, to reflect this, he is named after the landscape itself: Heathcliff *is* Wuthering Heights. In his book *Literature and Evil*, Georges Bataille wrote that there was an 'intimate connection' between hypermortality and the 'transgression of moral law' in Brontë's novel, which, for him, was 'the ultimate meaning of *Wuthering Heights*'. Extra-human life, death and the evocation of place are one in the novel.

> '*Landscape begins when it absorbs and dissolves all presences into itself.*'
>
> JEAN-LUC NANCY

It is clearly in your favour if the setting of your novel is familiar to you, but many writers starting out may opt not to write about the place they are most familiar with. David Almond has said how, for years as a writer, he completely avoided writing about the place in which he grew up – Tyneside – setting his novels instead 'in the garden suburbs of Surrey, on the surface of Mars, in the Australian outback'. He goes on to describe the Sunday market that was held on Newcastle's quayside, to which his grandfather used to take him. He says, 'There were fortune-tellers, quacks, masseurs, strongmen, almanac-sellers, acrobats, racing tipsters, buskers, magicians, card-sharps.' In particular, he remembers a strongman who 'stabbed himself with needles, whacked himself with metal bars, broke free from straitjackets and chains', and who afterwards would sneer and say, 'Pay! Get yer money out and pay!' When Almond started writing a book about an escapologist, he avoided using any of these childhood memories and produced a book that was 'strange, long-winded and aimless'. Only when he decided to base his main character on the man from the quayside market did the book come to life.

Even if you do know the setting for your novel very well, it is still a good idea to do some research into the area: locally produced guide books, council street plans, local libraries are all great sources of information and detail. Walking around an area to get a sense of the place is vital, too. My novel *The Mirror* is set in Venice and, although I know the city well, I made sure to revisit it when I was writing the book. It was incredibly helpful to see again the light on the water, the lovely pink and sand colours of the stones, but I made sure that the reader only experienced these things through the eyes of the main character, Oliva. It is the 'truth' of a place you are after, not the conveyance of information. The temptation is to describe, describe, describe, but the reader will be much more connected to your setting if it is evoked *because of* what the characters are seeing or doing rather than *in spite of* them. What you are after is a kind of fusion between character and setting. Make it feel like your character is 'touching' the setting and your reader will be there.

What you are after is a kind of fusion between character and setting

Use specific nouns whenever possible – nouns identify a place, verbs energise it and adjectives colour it. Is a house Georgian or Victorian, is the tree an ash or an oak, is the flower an aster or a daisy, exactly what shade of red? The reader will be situated and rooted in your setting if you provide them with such particular features. They act as portals into the imagination for the reader. As with creating a convincing character, less is more – a specific detail that is eye-catching and unique to that place will recreate a sense of place better than any amount of general description.

> 'The environment can act on the subject only to the extent that he comprehends it; that he transforms it into a situation. Hence no objective description of this environment could be of any use to us.'
>
> JEAN-PAUL SARTRE

Sartre suggests making no separation between self and world when describing setting. In this psychological landscape (*le paysage intérieur*), everything connects to, and is an expression of, a state of mind. Another French writer, Guy Debord, developed the concept of 'psychogeography', by which he meant that a writer should map a place via 'zones of feeling' rather than geographical features. In *Wuthering Heights*, for example, the window through which Heathcliff repeatedly sees Catherine's ghost is a 'zone of feeling'. The window represents a 'threshold' for him between life and death. Whenever he reaches for Catherine, she disappears. They can only be reunited in death, by him passing metaphorically through the window. Another example would be the short passage cited in the section on 'Telling' about the woman walking along the shore of a lake. For her, the lake is a 'lake of sorrow', a 'zone of feeling' for her absent son.

The idea of 'psychogeography' or 'zones of feeling' is one of the defining characteristics of existential literature, which sought to articulate a character's sentient self through the landscape around them. Think of Meursault, in Camus' *The Outsider*, as he steps onto the white sand beach: 'The sun was crashing down onto the sea and the sand and shattering into little pieces.' When he is handed the gun, the sun 'glinted off it' and 'the whole beach was reverberating in the sun and pressing against me from behind'. At the decisive moment, when Meursault is about to shoot the Arab, he says, 'All I could feel were the cymbals the sun was clashing against my forehead . . . The sea swept ashore a great breath of fire. The sky seemed to be splitting from end to end and raining down sheets of flame.' This example of Camus' famous 'white prose' is stripped down, connective and direct, and conveys character through landscape supremely well.

Try this: think about the house you grew up in and its environs. What was it like? How big was your house? Was it terraced or detached? What was it like on the outside? Was it stuccoed or open brickwork? Pebble-dash? Think back to your childhood bedroom and place yourself back in it as a child. Try to remember the size of it, the wallpaper, furniture, the smells, the sounds in the house and from outside, too, and write about it. Now imagine yourself in bed, ill. Rewrite your description of the bedroom with that in mind. How does that detail affect the environment around you?

Historical fiction
What is 'exposition' and how do we handle it?

'History is what's left in the sieve when the centuries have run through it – a few stones, scraps of writing, scraps of cloth.'

HILARY MANTEL

The British public loves reading historical novels. It is a common mistake to think that writers of historical fiction are really any different to writers of other kinds of fiction – you have the same issues to consider, the same tasks to overcome – but if you want to write a novel set in a particular period of history, your first and foremost task is obviously to try to recreate the time and place in your book as convincingly as possible. And that means you will need to do a lot of research. And that is fine, for research can often be one of the most pleasurable and rewarding parts of writing a novel. Spending months in a library locating, gathering, reading and collating notes can turn you into a kind of literary detective. Finding clues, following up on leads, stumbling upon hitherto unknown detail that, in turn, reveals further clues – this is all deeply satisfying and worthwhile. How you use all this research, all these facts and information, however, is another matter.

Exposition

Notwithstanding all the aspects of fiction we have looked at so far, one of the most important tasks you face as an author of historical fiction is to incorporate any social, cultural or political information into the fabric of the narrative as seamlessly as possible. Take this example from Simon Mawer's MAN Booker-shortlisted novel *The Glass Room*:

> She examines the garden elevation, a long, lean rectangle laid sideways across the page and crossed with vertical lines, a rectilinear universe that might have been designed by the new painter whom Rainer talked about, the Dutchman Mondrian.

The question here is, how likely is it that the character would think 'the Dutchman Mondrian' to themselves? Is it not the case that the narrator is putting that information into a character's thoughts in an unnatural way so that we get it? The character and Rainer have clearly had a conversation about 'the Dutchman Mondrian', and so they would both know very well who Rainer was referring to.

Rather than revealing anything about the person speaking, it feels as though someone else's words have been put into their mouth in order for the reader to understand exactly what the narrator wants. Information outside the parameters of the story that is placed into a narrative in this way, either by the narrator intruding directly into the story or by the narrator placing information into the mouths or minds of the characters, is called 'exposition'.

Exposition can sound and feel unnatural because the narrator is being allowed to impart information *directly* to the reader, thus bypassing character and story altogether. This device can struggle to ring true because it is there purely for the reader's benefit, not the characters', and it draws attention to the fact that the author has been unable to integrate character successfully into their historical context. Then again, for many readers, picking up historical detail in this way is one of the joys of historical fiction. At the end of the day, it's simply a matter of taste. But here I want to talk about trying to convey historical detail by channelling and funnelling it *through* character.

Instrumental, not incidental

> 'The writer's job is to recreate the texture of lived experience: to activate the senses, and to deepen the reader's engagement through feeling.'
>
> HILARY MANTEL

When writing historical fiction, try to ensure any historical detail is 'flush' with the narrative fabric, so that things happen *because of* the character's presence, not *in spite of* it. Characters should be instrumental in the telling of the story, not incidental to it. Historical fiction must be story-driven and internally coherent if it is going to avoid becoming ventriloquism or 'historical tourism'. We see, for example, what the streets of medieval London look like only when a character walks through them and sees those things for themselves. It is very tempting to start scenes with long, verbose descriptions of interiors, furnishings, decoration, clothing, but we will notice these things much more keenly if we see them through a character's eyes. It should be the very presence of the main character that determines historical events and background detail, not *vice versa*.

Characters should be instrumental in the telling of the story, not incidental to it

This issue relates back to an earlier point regarding the passivity of a character. When writing a historical novel, if you do not ensure that all the historical events are channelled and funnelled through character, these two elements can remain divorced from each other throughout the entire novel. In a poorly written historical novel, it is symptomatic that very little actually happens to characters directly because of the historical context. In a novel set during the Second World War, say, it is often the case that, when you sit down and consider it, no great change is actually brought about within any of the major characters *because of* the wartime setting. A book can be full of the drama of the mid-twentieth century, but it is the times themselves that change more than the characters. War rages in the background while your characters remain in the foreground, forever separated from these events, untouched by them.

The thought of including all your research can be seductive and very beguiling. You have expended so much effort in gathering this information and you do not want to let any of it go to waste, so you convince yourself that all of it is necessary. Pride gets in the way. You are determined to show the reader how much research you have done, and so you go about trying to impress them by piling up facts and information. Rather than bringing them into the story, however, all you are doing is pushing them away. They want to read a story, not be lectured at.

The best advice I was ever given on the subject was that, by all means, do as much research as you like, spend months and months on it if you wish, but once you start writing, make sure to forget all about it. Put it clear out of your mind and only refer to it if you are unsure of a detail. The historical setting of your novel should be part of your gut instinct just as much as any other aspect of writing, so let it sink down to that level before you start writing. Your job is not to 'write up' the researched material, but to nail the story itself, because you are writing a piece of imaginative fiction, not a book on history.

Potted history

The same is true when you provide expositional background information on the characters themselves. Traditionally, background detail like this has been communicated to the reader as a summary. Many classic nineteenth-century novels begin with, or have somewhere near their beginning, a potted history of a character's background. Chapter 1 of

Mary Shelley's *Frankenstein*, for example, begins, 'I am by birth a Genevese; and my family is one of the most distinguished of that republic. My ancestors had been for many years counsellors and syndics; and my father had filled several public situations with honour and reputation.'

This convention was challenged by the Modernists and has been challenged by writers ever since. Ford Madox Ford, for instance, suggested that a 'lumped' summary like this should be dropped in favour of a 'chronological looping'. *Vis-à-vis* the main character in a book, Ford stated that the writer ought to 'get him in first with a strong impression, and then work backwards and forwards over his past'. Following Ford's suggestion, any background information should be 'sprinkled' along the narrative, as and when it is needed, rather than being 'front-ended', all dumped at the beginning. Such distribution of background detail feels more organic because it arises naturally out of the story, instead of being mechanically dropped in as a block of summary.

When you look back over what you have written, whether it be researched historical detail, exposition in the form of narratorial comment or dialogue between characters, or background information as lumped summary, the question you have to ask yourself is the same – is this information absolutely necessary to push the story forward? Is the detail about that lovely earthenware cup glazed in gorgeous amber ochre really necessary? What about that page-long description of the gules and azure of the Duke

Do not stop to admire the scenery

of Norfolk's flag? You love these details in your narrative, so they are the moments about which you have to be the most brutally honest with yourself. Do not stop to admire the scenery – if setting is not conveyed because of a character's presence, or if it is not pushing the story forward, it is expendable, put in merely to please yourself. Kill your darlings. Write the *story*, not the history.

Life writing
How do we give life to historical people?

Fictional biography

> 'History is nothing other than a distillation of rumour.'
>
> THOMAS CARLYLE

Before I wrote *The Red Dancer*, I had no idea who Mata Hari was. I thought of her in the same way that I thought of Rasputin, or Madame Blavatsky – she was a 'name', yes, but why? What did she do to make herself so famous? I started researching the life of Mata Hari in the summer of 1998 by reading all the biographies of her life I could lay my hands on in the old British Library Reading Room, with its beautiful blue-domed ceiling. As I read them, I found that they all contradicted each other, and so I thought I could not trust any of them. But, crucially, they all had one thing in common: there seemed to be two keys to understanding her life – personal reinvention and self-delusion. How strongly we identify with historical figures depends on the idea of singleness and consistency – the more singular and consistent they are in the way they live their lives, the more 'knowable' they become (think of Einstein, Churchill or Gandhi) – but the life of Mata Hari was neither singular nor consistent; quite the contrary.

Rather than let that stop me from writing the book, though, I decided to see if I could structure *The Red Dancer* around this problem of who exactly Mata Hari was. I eventually arrived at the idea that the narrative could be a series of multiple and inconsistent points of view, made up of eyewitness accounts by people both real and imagined, mixed together with letters, newspaper cuttings, documents, quotations, interviews both real and imagined, as well as fiction.

My idea was that each of these chapters, narrated by people who encountered Mata Hari, would be discrete entities that, taken together, would paint a fuller picture of Mata Hari in a way that no single viewpoint could. But each of these narrators would not know that their testimony was part of a larger picture. They were not narrating with an agenda; they were just telling their story. The only character who does not have a voice in the book (except in the Prologue) is Mata Hari herself. Living in the public eye as she did, and in such a male-dominated world, her life was not entirely her own to control or keep. This is the real sadness in the story. In some ways, I think of Mata Hari as a proto-feminist but, at times, she was also her own worst enemy. Ultimately, my aim was not to take up a position for or against Mata Hari; rather, I wanted to present enough material for the reader to judge for themselves. After all, as Carlyle's quotation points out, history itself is nothing other than contesting stories, and the different stories surrounding the myth of Mata Hari are what lie at the heart of *The Red Dancer*.

Memoir/(auto)biography

'For most of history, anonymous was a woman.'

VIRGINIA WOOLF

Virginia Woolf famously described biography as 'a bastard, impure art' but, despite her protestations, the form has flourished for hundreds of years. With its emphasis on scholarliness, sources and cross-referencing, a biography is an attempt to adhere to the cradle-to-grave facts of a person's life, but, as any biographer knows, the 'truth' of a person can prove elusive. Worse still, the truth of a person and the facts of their life often do not match.

Fictional biography, with its distance between author and subject, can be classified as a type of life writing, but the term also includes memoirs, biographies and autobiographies, all of which imply a closer relationship between author and subject. While seemingly similar, the terms 'memoir' and 'biography' are, in fact, deceptively different. 'Memoir' does not claim to be the truth; it is, rather, an 'impression' of history, one that does not confuse clarity with accuracy. Memoirs have increasingly employed fictional techniques to tell their stories and, in doing so, they render those stories much more immediately than the driest kind of biography, which sticks doggedly to the facts. A good example of such a memoir is *Borrowed Finery* by Paula Fox.

When it comes to fictionalising a life, you become many things at once: historian, biographer, archivist, literary detective. If you are writing about a family member, however, your role as a relative must come last if the piece is to make a first impression on anyone outside your family. Be warned, though – when it comes to writing about yourself, or about a member of your family, all critical perspective can fly out the window and the story can stall, fail or collapse. Ethically and morally, it is a very grey area and so much is personally at stake, so there are a few important things to bear in mind.

— While researching, keep detailed notes. When you come to the actual writing, the small details will stand out. It is the small, personal details – especially 'qualia' – that will bring your characters to life and make your piece universal. In her memoir *Borrowed Finery*, Paula Fox describes her auntie's room in a residential home as having a smell 'composed of tobacco, mothballs, and the cough drops she sucked between cigarettes'. The detail says it all.

— Try to be as familiar with your material as possible, almost as if you were learning it by heart. Do as much research as you want, but when it comes to the actual writing, try to forget all about it. Be true to the spirit, not the letter.

Be true to the spirit, not the letter

— When you begin writing, be selective. You have to be judicious in your choice of action, incident and detail, and you have to combine these with skill and care. Try to find a common theme in the wealth of your material – this will eventually become the story. The commonality of theme – the through-line – will carry your reader.

— You can, perhaps, include yourself as the narrator,

someone to guide the reader through the story, as Edmund de Waal did in his memoir *The Hare with Amber Eyes*. If you take this approach, the way you respond to the unfolding story reveals yourself as a character and adds an extra layer of interest and complexity to the story.

— While what you are doing is, strictly speaking, neither fiction nor non-fiction, use fictional techniques in the telling of your story. Unlike stories, life does not have a strong structure or general themes, so you will have to impose these onto your material. Devices like building suspense, switching points of view, foreshadowing or unreliable narration can generate enormous power in your story, which perhaps, may otherwise struggle to keep the reader's attention.

In recent years, writers have also looked at things other than real historical characters to find good stories. Writers have turned to scientific discoveries, animals, minerals and plants, or single historic events as subjects for books – *Longitude* by Dava Sobel, *Cod* and *Salt*, both by Mark Kurlansky, *The Tulip* by Anna Pavord and Antony Beevor's *Stalingrad*, for example. By applying fictional techniques in the telling of these stories, we have a new 'hybridisation' of fiction and authentic social history. In combining these genres, we have a new unclassifiable form, one in which social history is more pleasurable to read and fiction is more knowledgeable.

This trend has grown to include memoirs that incorporate into their story some kind of cultural, natural or scientific interest of the author's. *H Is for Hawk*, for example, is a memoir by Helen Macdonald that deals with her grieving process and which is at the same time a falconer's diary. Likewise, Amy Liptrot's memoir *The Outrun* documents her chaotic twenties in London and subsequent return to her native Orkney after she gets sober, where she reconnects with the landscape and wildlife. Maggie Nelson's *Bluets* is ostensibly a book about her lifelong obsession with the colour blue, but it ends up discussing the painful end of an affair and the grievous injury of a dear friend.

Editing
A book is not written, but rewritten

So, you have finished your first draft. Congratulations! It is quite an achievement. You have come a long way and you have already succeeded where many others have failed. Enjoy the moment and have a well-earned rest. Then, when you think you are ready to return to the beginning of your book to start the editing process, do not do anything of the kind. Put your novel away and do not look at it again for as long as you possibly can. When she had finished a first draft, Jane Austen used to lock the manuscript in a drawer and give the key to a friend, with the instruction not to return it to her for one year, no matter how much she asked for it.

Put your novel away and do not look at it again for as long as you possibly can

So, pat yourself on the back, put your feet up, go out with friends, have a holiday. There will come a time when you feel ready to return to your draft. No one can say when this will be. For William Carlos Williams, it was the moment when 'the conditions under which it was written' had been forgotten. When you do eventually pull your draft out and have another look at it, the work will not have changed, but you will have. The white heat of creativity will have cooled and you now have a clear, cold eye on the work.

'Longer I can stay away before I have to get it to you the better it will be as [it] gives me a whole new chance to see it cold and plug any gaps and amplify where there is any need.'

ERNEST HEMINGWAY

They say a book is not written, but rewritten. That is true, and it means that editing can seem very daunting at first, but try not to think of the work ahead as an 'obstruction'. The most difficult part of writing is getting the first draft done, so the hardest part is behind you. Writing a first draft feels rather like driving at night from London to Birmingham – it is dark, you can see ahead of you only as far as the head-lights shine and you have no idea how long the journey will take, but you know that if you keep going in the right general direction, you will get there eventually.

Although it might have been based on some kind of plan, a first draft is still usually written more organically than mechanically. Coleridge talked about a well of consciousness into which everything is dropped, and the act of creation is lowering a bucket and pulling up words and images. Dredging the unconscious in this manner and including anything that is dragged to the surface means that first drafts are full of the language you are most familiar with, but which probably does not quite convey the thoughts, feelings and ideas you meant. You are at the mercy of a first draft while writing it, but when it is finished, the balance of power shifts in your favour. From the second draft onwards is when you can start to ensure that your long piece is as you intended. Editing, revising and shifting material is when the book, hopefully, will assume its natural shape and will come alive. This is Walter Benjamin's 'textile' phase.

The first person you should be writing for is yourself. You should be writing the kinds of books you would like to read, but once the first draft is finished, you have to start considering other people. Writing is for yourself, but rewriting is for others. The purpose of editing is not only to ensure that your long piece is as you intended, it is also to address the needs of your 'implied reader'. When you edit, you are asking them a series of questions, such as: 'Does this make sense to you?'; 'Do I need more here?'; 'Am I going too fast?'; 'Does it all add up?' The answers your implied reader gives you will be a good marker to work from. So, the editing process is a kind of paradox – it is a way of making your long piece truly your own, but it is also a way of bringing other people into the equation.

Writing is for yourself, but rewriting is for others

When you are ready to start the editing process, the first thing to do is to read your first draft. Do not make any notes as you read, and do not start editing – just read it. Resisting this impulse to start editing is crucial, because it is only when you finish reading the complete first draft that you will know where best to start the editing. A printed version is better than reading it onscreen. Even better is putting your work into some kind of book format. Whenever I have finished a first draft, I use an online book-printing service to make a bound, paperback copy for myself. I have found that reading it in the format for which it is intended gives me critical distance and clarity. If you do this, however, make only one copy and do not show it to anyone, and destroy it when you have finished with it. Before reading the book, it is also a good idea to take yourself out of the environment in which you wrote it. This will help you arrive at Williams' suggested state of forgetfulness. Go to a café, the park or a friend's house for the weekend. A change of scenery will re-energise you and give you even more clarity.

> 'A true poet does not bother to be poetical. Nor does a gardener bother to scent his roses.'
>
> JEAN COCTEAU

The most common pattern by far for all writers is to write a lot and then edit the material down, and we have seen that new writers tend to be guilty of overwriting. This is the result of 'trying too hard' and indicates a loss of nerve on their part, a failure to trust the reader's imagination. It is often at key dramatic moments in the plot that a writer loses confidence and relinquishes control over the narrative. The moment a firm hand is needed to keep the story on course is the very moment new writers relax their grip and the story wobbles. Rather than trusting the characters and the story to speak for themselves, the new writer tends to 'wade in' with all kinds of overwrought, over-the-top effects in an effort to ensure that the reader understands the significance of the moment. Instead of *showing* a character's excess, the writer steps in and desperately *insists* that the character is excessive. The resultant prose can be very purple indeed.

At key dramatic moments – a drastic role reversal, an exchange of guilt, a dramatic announcement, a long-dead hero making an unexpected comeback, a death, a birth, a car chase or a knock on the door – have faith in your characters and story and resist the urge to pre-empt the reader's enjoyment of these by having the narrator intervene and go overboard in their description, or by adding 'portent', or by being vague about how people feel. If properly constructed, the drama in a scene should be perfectly able to speak for itself without the writer gilding the lily. Readers are sophisticated people and will deeply resent any form of manipulation or patronisation on the narrator's part. As ever, less really is more – let them make up their own minds as to what they should understand and how they should be feeling.

When you have finished reading your draft, read it again, this time making edits, notes, suggestions on the manuscript. At this stage, try not to be too harsh in your judgements. Remember, first drafts are just starting points – really, they should be called 'zero' drafts – and are always messy. Allow for that. The key to good editing is to do draft after draft, and you will not be able to see in one sitting all that needs to be done.

Look at the plot in general. What happens when you move from one scene to another? Is there forward movement, a momentum? Does the story sustain itself and develop? Do you find events surprising? Are there any holes that need filling? Do you find yourself wondering what happens to such-and-such a character? Perhaps you need to flesh out their story? Are there any loose ends? Do you resolve the characters' dilemmas to a degree that will satisfy the reader but that also leaves room for their own interpretation?

When you are more or less happy with the overall content and placement of scenes, move from the general to the specific and look at them individually. What kind of shape are they in? Do you satisfy the objective of each scene? Does the action in the scene say something about the characters? Is it moving too fast? Too slow? Is it pushing the story forward? Is it doing too much, or too little? If you left it out, would the story be lacking something?

> *'For if the presence or absence of something makes no apparent difference, it is no real part of the whole.'*
>
> ARISTOTLE

If you hit a wall in the editing process, a moment when you simply do not know what is wrong with a scene or how to resolve it, nine times out of ten it is the result of weak plotting or weak characterisation.

When he thought he had finished writing *The Great Gatsby*, for instance, F. Scott Fitzgerald was dissatisfied with how short it was – 50,000 words. Rather than being too short, the story was in reality slightly underdeveloped and Fitzgerald's editor encouraged him to fill it out. Fitzgerald went back to work, splicing in an extra 10,000 words here and there. The 60,000-word version is the one we have today and is one of the most perfect novels ever written. So, if you feel the story is underbaked, go back to the planning stage and look again at your story and plot. Do you need to add one or two scenes? Perhaps you need to lengthen some chapters, or cut others completely and write new ones?

'Similes are like defective ammunition.'
ERNEST HEMINGWAY

Cut down your scenes to their bare bones. Ensure they make their point but do not outstay their welcome. Then look at the writing line by line. Although each scene needs to serve the story, it should also be as beautifully written as possible in itself. Does each sentence stand up well on

Cut down your scenes to their bare bones.

its own? When you place two sentences side by side, is there an attraction between them? Do the sentences align themselves to each other? Do they flow well together? Is there a pleasing mix of long and short sentences? Does this create a rhythm? If any sentence seems too long, it almost certainly is – break it in two and see if they both fit in somewhere. If not, cut one. Work on your sentences until they feel finished, and then polish the words until they shine.

Adjectives are like coins – spend them wisely. Assigning more than two adjectives to a noun causes us to lose sight of the object, rather than bringing it into sharp focus.

Cut words such as 'suddenly', 'immediately', 'gradually', 'eventually', 'particularly', 'practically', 'probably', 'apparently', 'absolutely', 'nearly', 'virtually', 'finally', 'usually', 'really', 'actually', 'almost', 'often', 'never', 'seem to', 'like', 'just', 'sort of', 'somehow', 'pretty', 'slightly', 'totally', 'fairly', 'quite'. Search for stronger, more distinct words. Be precise. Avoid retreating into abstraction, especially those abstract nouns that describe states of feeling. All we have for a character whose heart has 'turned to stone' is your word for it. We need to see the emotion for ourselves. Be concrete. Show, don't tell.

> *'Adverbs are a mortal sin.'*
>
> ELMORE LEONARD

Another common trap for new writers to fall into is relying too much on adverbs. The problem here is that, as with the use of cliché, exposition or unintentional 'telling', the use of adverbs is the moment when a writer takes the easy, lazy route. It seems fine to use adverbs, they appear to fit seamlessly into the writing but, in fact, they only draw attention to themselves. They are moments when the story jumps out of its groove. Relying overly on adverbs means that you are avoiding the real work of a writer, which is to find the most interesting and dramatic way to get an idea across.

Take this example: '"Get your hands off me!" Clarenceux snarled angrily.' You have a triple whammy here – not only is anger implied in the line of dialogue (an imperative complete with a back-up exclamation mark!), but 'to snarl' also implies 'anger', and then, to top it all off, there is the adverb 'angrily', which is redundant. The use of the adverb here does not add any greater power to the line of dialogue – indeed, it only serves to diminish its impact. Adverbs tend to impoverish verbs, not empower them. And they are crafty. Like cliché, exposition or unintentional 'telling', adverbs are moments when the writer has 'switched off' and has become blind to their writing self. They act as a kind of shorthand for the real work ahead. But remember, first drafts are just nuts and bolts of story plus 'notes to self' like these, so do not worry: drafting and editing is the time when you can shake your manuscript free of them all.

First drafts are just nuts and bolts of story plus 'notes to self'

As you work with the conscious part of your brain, issues will also be resolved in your unconscious. As you shape and shift your material, you will find yourself thinking about it all the time, at the unlikeliest of moments. In a bar, listening to a friend, an idea for a particular scene will pop into your head. Gazing out the window on a bus, you will stumble across the solution to something that has been evading you for weeks. Have a notebook with you at all times when you are away from your desk and write down straightaway every editorial suggestion that comes to mind.

Do not leave it till later – write it down now, or else you will surely forget it.

Editing can be the most satisfying, creative part of the whole writing process, the period when your mind is working simultaneously on both micro and macro levels. Unexpectedly, you might even find yourself coming up with ideas for new projects. François Truffaut said that when he was writing a screenplay, he could not wait to direct it, and that when he was directing it, he was looking forward to editing it, and that when he was in the editing room, all he could think about was writing again. The end of one project can be a launching pad for another. The entire writing process is cyclical.

The things wrong with a novel are just invitations for you to make it better. If you are good, you know you can be better. But at what point do you know when to stop? The first thing to ask yourself is whether or not you have said what you wanted to say. If you did not know what you wanted to say in the first place, how will you know you are finished? Just as it is perfectly possible not to edit a book sufficiently, so it is possible to overdo it. All good books are more than the sum of their parts. They have something ineffable about them, a quality that must not become a casualty of the editing process. So, when do you let go?

You will know when you are finished, believe me. I realise that this will sound frustrating to a new writer, but it is as simple as that. Endings of novels are 'felt' rather than logically thought out. The key to making a novel better is to revise continually, moving with due care and attention through successive drafts like the beam of a lighthouse. Print out, read, edit, revise, print out. At first, this work might entail some major structural rejigging; eventually it will come down to tightening one or two scenes. But there will come a time when all you are doing is minor tweaking, fine-tuning a few words here and there. You cannot find any more obvious passages to cut or places to rework. The book is resisting your efforts, telling you to leave it alone. You realise that the book you now have in front of you is very similar to what you originally had in mind. Your desire to make changes wanes. You are very near the end now.

I am a strong believer that things can always be made better, but that perfection can never be reached. Novels are 'perfectible', in the sense that there can be perpetual improvement, but 'perfectible' does not mean 'made perfect'. A novel is never finished, only ever abandoned. If we arrived at perfection, there would be no further room for improvement, so attaining perfection is a kind of death. The book in front of you is similar to what you had in mind, but not exactly the same. This is as good as it gets.

A novel is never finished, only ever abandoned.

If you are striving to write the perfect novel, stop now, because you never will and you have to make your peace with that. You have to relinquish responsibility at some point; beyond that point lie monsters. Although your book will never be exactly as you had imagined, that does not mean that you will not be impressed by what you have achieved. Ideas come and go, you plan and initiate many projects, but the returns are diminishing and sometimes unlooked for. It turns out that what you end up with is richer and stranger than you intended. You leap back in surprise at what is before you. 'This is plenty,' you think, 'this is more than enough.' Time to put down your pen and walk away.

Afterword
Books are mirrors, whether we write them or read them

'Only bad writers think their work is really good.'

ANNE ENRIGHT

Stories help us to understand ourselves. Life hurls random, chaotic events at us from all directions and the only way we can make sense of it all is by assimilating those events into our own personal narrative – the constant dialogue we have with ourselves, asking what such-and-such means, how it compares to a similar event, how we feel and what we will do about it, if anything. As events accumulate, we continually construct and reconstruct our life story, we find comparisons and contrasts with previous memories and alter our expectations and ambitions for the future. Writing is an extension of the thought process and of living; it is the necessary response to the condition of life. Our lives are made of bits

Our lives are made of bits and pieces, and writing is stitching them together

and pieces, and writing is stitching them together. The act of putting together stories helps to tell us where and how we fit into the world. We are always looking to make sense of the world and we will impose a simulacrum of order onto it whenever possible. When we wake each morning, we remake the world. We do this every day.

Writing a novel takes this personal narrative and finds what T. S. Eliot calls an 'objective correlative' for it, 'a set of objects, a situation, a chain of events which shall be the formula of that *particular* emotion'. You have done that – your novel sits before you. When you think about it, your novel catches you in its headlights. It surprises you, like glancing in the mirror and, for a moment, not recognising yourself. It is an unsettling sensation, but also appealing. You are not quite sure which way to look.

You will almost certainly feel emotionally exhausted after finishing your novel. All that transference of emotion and energy can leave you feeling depleted. But your book is alive, which is the main thing. The trust you have placed in your imagination and your intuition has produced this magical, improbable, baffling object in front of you. You have made your mark on the world, your *cri de coeur* has been heard. The book is yours, but it is ours now, too. We have been swept up by its narrative pull and have been touched by its emotional involvement. You have made the personal universal.

> 'And, by the way, everything in life is writable about if you have the outgoing guts to do it, and the imagination to improvise. The worst enemy to creativity is self-doubt.'
>
> SYLVIA PLATH

Now that you have finished your book and the gut instincts that drove you to write it in the first place have turned to butterflies in your stomach, what next? If you are planning on sending your novel out, prepare yourself – the publishing industry is a harsh one. When you are writing a book, you are an artist, but when it comes to trying to publish it, you have to become a businessman or woman. Remember that any criticism agents or publishers offer is subjective and not personal. Unhitch your self-esteem from your publishing track record. Develop a thick skin, but remain open to their ideas. Draw on the positives.

Whatever your next step is, there will hopefully come a time when you find that something else pops into your mind and keeps bothering you, like a stone in your shoe. It could be that bizarre story you heard at a dinner six months ago, or an image from a novel that has left a deep impression. This is the first inkling of the next book beginning to evolve in the back of your mind. If you are ready, able and willing to experience the frustration, elation, hard graft, inspiration, perplexity and satisfaction all over again, then you could be about to begin the whole process once more. Now could be the opportunity to do an even better job, for every novel is an attempt at correcting the failings of the previous one.

Writing is a discipline with no end in sight, and writers never really retire. We write books in order to make sense of our lives and to show the reader some aspect of their own lives that had hitherto remained undisclosed. Books are mirrors, whether we write them or read them. In the end, it is all part of the same process. Having written your book will fill you with joy and wonder, but you will also feel anxiety as it makes its way in the world. How will it fare? What can you do to help? You have very little control over this stage. You have loosed your arrow and now have to wait and see where it falls. Support your book when it is down, revel in its success when it is up, but remember: success and failure are both imposters. The work is all; it is we who walk away.

Essays referred to and recommended

Aristotle; 'Ars Poetica' in *Aristotle/Horace/Longinus: Classical Literary Criticism*, trans. by T. S. Dorsch (Penguin, 1965)

Auster, Paul; *The Art of Hunger* (Faber & Faber, 1998)

Barthes, Roland; 'The Death of the Author' in *Image-Music-Text* (Macmillan, 1977)

Bazin, André; *What Is Cinema?* Vol. 1, trans. by H. Gray (University of California Press, 1967)

Bettelheim, Bruno; *The Uses of Enchantment* (Penguin, 1991)

Bowen, Elizabeth; 'Notes on Writing a Novel' (Orion II, 1945)

Bowles, Paul; *Conversations with Paul Bowles*, ed. by Gena Dagel Caponi (University Press of Mississippi, 1993)

Bresson, Robert; *Notes on the Cinematographer* (Quartet Encounters, 1986)

Chatman, Seymour; *Antonioni, or the Surface of the World* (University of California Press, 1985)

Chatman, Seymour; *Story and Discourse: Narrative Structure in Fiction and Film* (Cornell University Press, 1978)

Eliot, T. S.; 'Traditional and the Individual Talent' in *The Sacred Wood: Essays on Poetry and Criticism* (Faber & Faber, 1997)

Field, Syd; *Screenplay: The Foundations of Screenwriting* (Bantam Doubleday Dell, 1998)

Hemingway, Ernest; *On Writing*, ed. by Larry W. Phillips (Granada, 1985)

Iser, Wolfgang; 'The reading process: a phenomenological approach' in *Modern Criticism and Theory*, ed. by David Lodge (Longman, 1988)

Jakobson, Roman; 'The metaphoric and metonymic poles' in *Modern Criticism and Theory*, ed. by David Lodge (Longman, 1988)

Kundera, Milan; *The Art of the Novel* (Faber & Faber, 1988)

Mamet, David; *On Directing Film* (Faber & Faber, 1991)

Nabokov, Vladimir; *Lectures on Literature* (Picador, 1983)

McQuillan, Martin (ed.); *The Narrative Reader* (Routledge, 2000)

Pollack, Sydney; 'Acting is Doing' in *Projections 3* (Faber & Faber, 1994)

Pound, Ezra; 'A Retrospect' in *Poetry in Theory: An Anthology 1900–2000*, ed. by Jon Cook (Blackwell Publishing, 2004)

Propp, Vladimir; 'Morphology of the Folktale' (University of Texas Press, 1968)

Robbe-Grillet, Alain; 'Riddles and Transparencies in Raymond Roussel' in *Raymond Roussel: Life, Death & Works* (Atlas Press, 1987)

Sayers, Dorothy L.; 'Aristotle on Detective Fiction' in *Unpopular Opinions* (Victor Gollancz, 1946)

Schrader, Paul; *Transcendental Style in Film*: Ozu, Bresson, Dreyer (Da Capo Press, 1972)

Shklovsky, Victor; 'Art as Technique' in *Modern Criticism and Theory*, ed. by David Lodge (Longman, 1988)

Sontag, Susan; 'Against Interpretation', 'On Style' and 'Spiritual style in the films of Robert Bresson' in *Against Interpretation* (Vintage, 2001)

Acknowledgements

Thanks to my former students who said some very kind things about this book: Dan Dalton, Chloé Esposito, Alice Feeney, Katie Khan, Renée Knight, Ali Land, Laline Paull, Lydia Ruffles & SJ Watson. Thanks to staff past and present who have helped to make Faber Academy what it is: Nicci Cloke, Joey Connolly, Becky Fincham & Catherine Heaney. Thanks to good Faber folk Andrew Benbow & Stephen Page for the music. Thanks to Kate Ward for typesetting the book. Thanks to my superagent, Clare Conville, without whom this book would not have been possible. A big thank you to my long-standing co-tutor, Joanna 'JayBeeze' Briscoe, for her friendship and many lunchtime hours spent together in Pret. A very special thank you to Director of Faber Academy, Ian Ellard, who edited this book beautifully. Lastly, to my dear departed friend Becky Swift, co-founder of The Literary Consultancy, who gave me my first big break.

The Thirty Steps

Over the years, I've found that most novels comprise around thirty key scenes. Use the slips overleaf to summarise your story, then play with the order to find the most effective plot

1

{ *cause and effect* }

2

{ *be patient, remain empty* }

3

{ *create something out of nothing* }

4

{ *is this a reversal?* }

5

{ *in late, out early* }

....

....

....

6

{ *make connections* }

....

....

....

7

a continual process of elimination }

....

....

....

8

sustain and develop }

....

....

....

9

the fulfilment of targets }

....

....

....

10

work your plot backwards }

11

....

....

....

{ *find the desire line* }

12

....

....

....

{ *the path of least resistance* }

13

....

....

....

{ *measure twice, cut once* }

14

....

....

....

{ *is this the donnée* }

15

....

....

....

{ *is this in the right place* }

16

{ aperture or closure? }

17

{ are you going to preserve chronology? }

18

whittle away the alternatives }

19

leave room for manoeuvre }

20

pace doesn't necessarily mean speed }

21

{ *is there conflict?* }

22

{ *the point of no return*

23

{ *what comes before?* }

24

{ *what comes after?*

25

{ *could you cut this*

{ *twist your plot like a screw* }

is there 'qualia'? }

what's your inciting incident? }

he current in the river }

s your ending surprising and inevitable? }

And there you have it. A novel. Now all that's left is to write the thing . . .